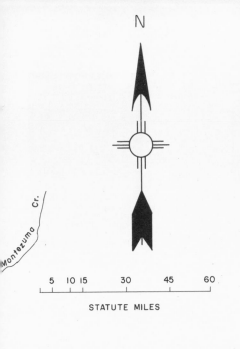

N

STATUTE MILES

5 10 15   30   45   60

OLORADO

NEW MEXICO

Animos R.

Shiprock

o Farmington

San   Juan   R.

TWO GRAY
o HILLS

RYSTAL

GALLUP

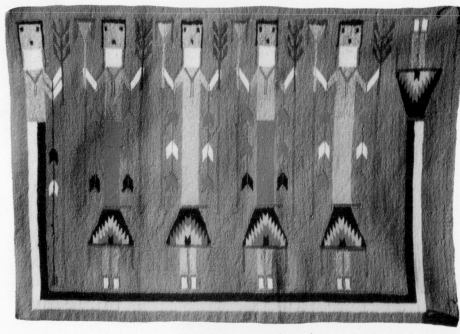

Shiprock–Lukachukai

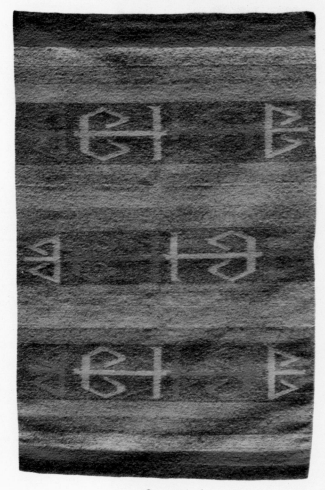

Crystal

Chinle

Posts and Rugs

The Story of Navajo Rugs and Their Homes

Navajo weaver and friend

Posts and Rugs

The Story of Navajo Rugs and Their Homes

by

H. L. James

**SOUTHWEST PARKS AND
MONUMENTS ASSOCIATION**

Box 1562, Globe, Arizona 85501

Preface

In 1934, Charles Avery Amsden ended his classic study on Navajo weaving by stating, *"This brief study of an aboriginal craft which became a modern industry cannot in full conscience close its pages without a glance ahead, for studies of the past have little value unless they serve in some measure to illumine the future. I see the immediate future of Navaho weaving as a race between two forces. One of these is the Americanization of the Navaho; the other is the education of the American to the Indian. They are mutually antagonistic; the first of them working against the future of our craft, the second for it. . . . How far has our appreciation of the Indian's art and craft progressed — is it far enough to offset the pull of this force and keep the woman at her loom by paying her a fair price for her work?. . . . Even in our growing sympathy for the Indian, a danger lurks, for America has ever assimilated most rapidly those alien groups to which the heartiest welcome was extended. Surely the end of it all is clearly enough in view. The only question remaining is: how long?"*[1]

Amsden wrote during the Revival Period of Navajo weaving, when a new level of excellence followed a decline in quality. Today, in the Regional Style Period, the craft, though not in a period of decline, is faced with uncertainty, and the race of Amsden's predicted forces will ultimately be won by the Americanization of the Navajo, which will force its eventual extinction. In view of this, a photographic record is of the utmost significance in establishing completeness of the craft, to illustrate the rug in its true definition of American Indian art. The visual impact of the contemporary Navajo rug is dynamic. The creative designs and colorful fibers convey the sensitivity of a remarkable people living in a remarkable land.

The information contained in the data sheets in Chapters 3 through 11 was compiled during frequent trips to the Navajo Reservation in 1969-73. The prices of rugs were brought up to date in late 1974. Names of the weavers were supplied by area Indian traders. They by no means represent the hundreds of experienced craftswomen who weave on the Reservation, but those who, in the opinion of the traders, are presently active in their region at this writing.

Available population figures at some of the trading posts reflect figures provided by the Navajo Tribe Statistics Bureau as of April 1, 1974.

In Appendix III, 1974 Navajo Weaving Awards, results from four exhibits are listed. Several other annual exhibits, whose awards listings were not available, include:

1. Arizona State Fair, Phoenix, Arizona.
2. Heard Museum, Phoenix, Arizona.
3. Museum of Northern Arizona, Flagstaff, Arizona.

Acknowledgments

This book is the result of a five year study, 1969 to 1974. I am deeply grateful to many people who contributed to the building of it. Most notably I am indebted to:

R. A. Pfeifer, of Albuquerque, for constructing the pattern sketches of the rug designs.

Donald J. Mills of Evanston, Illinois, for the pencil renderings in Chapter 2.

Bill Young, the amiable trader at Hubbell Trading Post, who helped in so many ways, including the necessary impetus to the publishers.

The National Park Service, and in particular Mr. Kevin McKibbin, then superintendent at Hubbell Trading Post National Historic Site, for making available accommodations in the guest hogan during my photographic stay at the post, a gesture truly in keeping with the hospitality of Juan Lorenzo.

Ginger and Jim Price, of Price's All Indian Shop, Albuquerque, for permission to photograph rug examples.

Ann and Manny Goodman, of the Covered Wagon, Albuquerque, for permission to photograph rug examples.

Edna Norton, of the latter's shop, for providing assistance.

Octavia Fellin, librarian at Gallup, for help in the research.

Martin Link, Director of the Navajo Tribal Museum at Window Rock, for research aids.

Noël Bennett, of Gallup, for technical review and suggestions to Chapter 2.

Dave Brugge, historian at Hubbell Trading Post for review and suggestions to the manuscript.

George Hight, Gallup photographer, for illustrations assistance.

Allan Reed of Tobe Turbin Trading Post, Gallup, for supplying various data.

Last, but certainly not least, to each of the very cooperative men who operate major trading posts in the nine regional style centers, for collaboration on their respective chapters, to wit:

Ed Foutz (Shiprock)
Bob French (Teec Nos Pos)
Derald Stock (Two Gray Hills)
Bill Young (Ganado)
Jerry Norris (Tonalea)

Kenneth Kennedy (Lukachukai)
Don Jensen (Crystal)
Gerald LaFont (Chinle)
John Rieffer (Wide Ruins)

Eugene, Oregon — April 16, 1975

the Author

H. L. James is senior engineering geologist with the New Mexico State Highway Department. He was raised on a ranch in southeastern New Mexico; attended schools in Carlsbad, Santa Fe, New Mexico; Hays, Kansas; and West Texas State University in Canyon, Texas; where he received his Bachelor of Science Degree in 1958. He is currently on a sabbatical doing graduate research at the University of Oregon. Mr. James has traveled the Navajo Reservation extensively during the past 15 years collecting examples of Navajo weaving. A past two-term Vice President of the New Mexico Historical Society, he is recognized for his writing and photography on Southwestern history and geology.

— The Publisher

Contents

List of Illustrations

SPECIALTY RUGS & OTHER TYPES

MAPS

CHARTS

Chapter 1

History

Much has been written on the history of Navajo weaving. It is generally agreed that the events of the craft are categorized into six periods of development: the Early Classic Period (1700-1850), Classic Period (1850-1863), Transition Period (1868-1890), Rug Period (1890-1920), Revival Period (1920-1940), and the Regional Style Period (1940-present).

Early Classic Period: 1700-1850

The wheels of Spanish exploration were set in motion with the advance of Coronado into the desert Southwest in 1540. The explorers brought with them herds of churro-type sheep and introduced them to the pueblo dwellers along the Rio Grande; hence the origin of wool preparation in the Southwest.

The Navajo learned the art of weaving from Pueblo Indians who fled into Navajo sanctuaries following the Revolt of 1680, although some of these skills may have been picked up from them somewhat earlier in the same century. Simple clothing was the main objective: women's dresses, men's shirts and breech cloths, shoulder blankets, leggings, belts, hair cords, and ponchos. Patterns were simple, primarily in narrow stripes and bands. Colors were mostly the natural wool tones of white, gray, brown, tan, and black. Some

vegetal dying was used in ranges of rust, yellow, and green. Indigo blue was introduced early by the Spanish and became widely used with natural yarns throughout the Early Classic Period.

Some trade in blankets to Spanish-Americans began on a small scale in the 1700's; also with the Pueblo Indians. During the latter part of the period, Spanish enslavement of the Navajos resulted in the first definitive style piece, the so-called "slave blanket." These fabrics, which were woven for their European masters on upright looms, exhibited both Spanish and Navajo characteristics.

Classic Period: 1850-1863

In the 150 years or so after they began weaving, the Navajo far surpassed their Pueblo teachers as suppliers of blankets for the Spanish, other Indians, and by 1850, to American traders and settlers. The Classic Period brought them increasing economic success. The shoulder blanket for men, distinctively patterned in broad black or blue and white horizontal bands, was changed by addition of diamond and check designs in red, sometimes yellow and green. This became the Chief Blanket, widely traded to United States military leaders, Ute, and other Indian warriors.

Patterns remained relatively simple, but there was great technical excellence in spinning

Bayeta, circa 1840. Reproduced from Hollister (1903), Plate VII.
(Courtesy: Gallup, New Mexico, Public Library).

Chief Blanket, circa 1865. Reproduced from Hollister (1903), Plate VI.
(Courtesy: Gallup, New Mexico, Public Library).

Germantown Eye-Dazzler, circa 1878. Reproduced from Hollister (1903), Plate IX.
(Courtesy: Gallup, New Mexico, Public Library).

Ganado, circa 1891. Reproduced from Hollister (1903), Plate V.
(Courtesy: Gallup, New Mexico, Public Library).

and weaving. Unable to produce brilliant red, the Navajo traded for bolts of English manufactured baize (a wool cloth called bayeta in Spanish).[2] The weavers unraveled the red fabric, respun the threads and used them in combinations with the native wool. American flannel, when available, was similarly used. Additional imports into the Southwest, through Spain, Mexico, and United States frontier routes, were the colorful pre-aniline, three-ply European yarns, generally called Saxony. The combination of bayeta red and indigo blue, with the distinctive sheens of Saxony, yielded highly marketable items. With new colors came inventiveness in design, such as terraced motifs, zigzags, diamonds, and outlined crosses.

By the early 1860's the golden age of weaving had arrived, but at its seemingly grandest hour, the textile revolution of the Classic Period tragically collapsed with the fall and imprisonment of the Navajo people.

Between the years 1863-1868, the United States Government "rounded up" and interned the Indians at Bosque Redondo (Round Grove) on the Pecos River in east-central New Mexico, for alleged raids against Mexican and American settlements. Deprived of native wool while in exile, the weavers turned to machine-made yarn supplied by their captors and continued to make blankets for sale.

Transition Period: 1868-1890

With their pacification, the Navajos were allowed to return to their beloved redrocks on June 18, 1868. With the trials and chaos of resettlement behind them, the freed weavers, now familiar with commercial yarn, slowly began to embark on a wild extravaganza of color. Bayeta and Saxony wools of the Classic Period were replaced after 1880 by a newly introduced yarn called Germantown. This was a coarse, four-ply and three-ply, aniline-dyed yarn, much of it manufactured in western Pennsylvania. At the height of Germantown use (1890) came a period of decline; poor workmanship, design carelessness, and gaudy color balances became the rule.[3] The commercial aspects of the craft drifted into confusion and aimlessness.

After the Civil War, a population influx swept the Southwest. With this growth came a new breed of man, the Indian trader, a unique type of individual who bridged the great gap between the red and white races. By the mid-1870's, government licensed traders were spreading across the Reservation, setting up remote outposts of goods, and personally concerning themselves with the problem of weaving. The imagination of the trader brought new stimulus to the craft. Goods sold by traders introduced the weavers to a new field of visual designs: the alphabet, patterns on supply sacks, pictures, and catalogs.

As the 20th century approached, the weaving industry slowly regained its balance. There were two main reasons for this change: (1) the trader and the development of regional styles of weaving; and (2) the transition from blanket to rug. Rugs were created when weavers stopped making blankets for themselves, turning instead to another trader provided item, the machine-made Pendleton blanket, as wearing apparel. There was still demand for Navajo fabrics, but what resulted was a new found market for heavier and larger weaves, supplying the white man with floor coverings. Commercial Germantown yarns generally lost favor with traders, and weavers turned to using handspun wool.

Rug Period: 1890-1920

By the early 1900's came the greatest rug market the industry had yet known, and production was soon pressed to keep up with demand.

Already important in the 1880's, commercial dyes were gaining a foothold on the Reservation, and the new colors gave greater intensity to the fine textiles that were being produced. New styles were experimented with, one of the most significant being the bordered rug.[4] The framed format was encouraged by traders for its appeal to eastern clientele. By 1920, few rugs left the loom without some form of outside band to enclose the pattern.

Two traders of the period, Juan Lorenzo Hubbell of Ganado, Arizona, and John B. Moore of Crystal, New Mexico, greatly influenced the growth of the craft. Hubbell demanded quality of his weavers, discouraging inferior dyes and loose woven fabrics. He encouraged a return to Classic Period designs: bold crosses, stripes, and diamonds which he set against a brilliant red aniline background

Juan Lorenzo Hubbell (seated) with rug displays. Hubbell Trading Post, circa 1890.
(Ben Wittick photo, courtesy: Photograph Collections, Museum of New Mexico).

bordered in black. He commissioned artists E. A. Burbank, Bertha A. Little, and others to paint rug patterns in oil and watercolor, and these samples were hung in his post for the weavers to copy. Hubbell also urged the weaving of heavier products — durable pieces in larger sizes to be used as area rugs in the home. In return, he promised his weavers higher sales in a greater market. The Fred Harvey Company stocked hundreds of the famed Ganado "reds" in their tourist outlets along the Santa Fe Railroad, and the rug became famous.

John B. Moore was also a disciple of craftsmanship. He had his weavers bring in raw wool which he then sent to eastern mills for machine cleaning and dyeing. When returned, the processed wool could be spun and woven more evenly. The technical quality of Moore-based rugs met with immediate success. He published a mail order catalog outlining grades of wool, classes of rugs, and

prices. This now out-of-print and rare booklet was illustrated with photographs of weavers at work, and contained the first color plates of Navajo rugs. Like Hubbell, Moore also employed an artist to set down design styles combining some traditional Navajo figures with some geometrics of his own imagination. His distinctive styles included a bordered rug with the natural wool tones of black, brown, and white coupled with carded blends of gray, tan, and beige, and used in combinations with commercial dyes of red and blue. Moore's greatest contribution was perhaps the designs that he originated. In the years to come, his basic patterns would give rise to a popular regional style rug called the Two Gray Hills.

Beginning in 1910, Navajo weaving started a descent into its second depression. During this time the U.S. Government, hoping to improve meat capacities of the tribe, introduced large flocks of French Rambouillet sheep to the Reservation. The new animal was a

7

Extra fine and perfectly cleaned, per piece, $10.00 to $50.00 each, according to size and quality.

I have no saddle blankets nor common ones to quote.

Any of the grade will be shipped on approval with the understanding that the customer assumes all transportation costs both ways in case of return; and that no deductions on this account be allowed from invoice price in case of acceptance. We will ship, prepay, allow deductions from invoice price, on the extra fine ones of this grade, priced per piece, just the same as on the "ER-20" class, but only on these, of this "T-XX" class.

A FEW HINTS FOR THE CUSTOMER IN ORDERING

You always get the best value for your money in the higher priced rugs. You will be, and must be, pleased in these, and are assured against the possibility of buying and paying for a thing not satisfactory, by the return privilege allowed on all fine rugs.

You get just the size, the colors, and the pattern wanted, if you order from the "ER-20" class. If it is not in stock when your order comes, and you are willing to allow us a reasonable time in which to have it done, we will have it made for you especially. In this way you get something exclusive without the least danger of any other ever having something just like it.

Do not order the best quality and stipulate the lowest price. We wish in all cases to give the best possible value for the money and know that we do it, but I nor no other can sell our best goods for our lowest prices.

(*Continued on page 25*)

By permission Sim. Schwemberger.

NAVAJO RUG IN THE MAKING—The finished job.
(Do you recognize the XXIV pattern?)

A sample page from *The Navajo* catalog. Photo: Top-of-the-line Crystal weaving, circa 1911. John B. Moore is shown with one of his weavers illustrating a ER-20 grade rug. Note the broad border, hook elements, and the central cross and diamond pattern — all characteristically Moore designs. (Courtesy: Gallup, New Mexico, Public Library).

good producer, both in mutton and fleece, but for weaving purposes it was a disaster. The new wool was short and oily, difficult to clean, card, spin, and weave. Rugs coming off the loom were heavy and coarse textured. The white patterns showed dirty gray casts. Bright colors were carelessly dyed and reflected a loss of brilliance. Weavers soon lost an interest in their work and designs became stereotyped. Prices and demand fell drastically. To stimulate production, traders began buying rugs by the pound. Weavers responded and began to weave the wool without eliminating grease and dirt, thus increasing its weight. Some weavers went to such extremes as to saturate their rugs with "rubbed-in" dirt. Penalites were imposed for this practice, but it could not be controlled. By 1920, a gloom of lost initiative had settled over the Reservation.

Revival Period: 1920-1940

As is generally the case in most individual endeavors, a period of deterioration is usually followed by one of distinction. Some dedicated person or persons takes on the task for reversing the tide and thus brings forth a new level transcending all previous efforts.

Several persons were responsible for the craft's second rejuvenation. Most notable was Leon H. McSparron, of Chinle Trading Post. In 1923, this trader, in association with a Navajo benefactress named Mary C. Wheelright, undertook a program to encourage weavers of that district to experiment with the old vegetal dye methods that were used prior to introduction of commercial colorants (1880). The Chinle weavers developed pastel plant hues of browns, golds, and greens in Early Classic Period patterns of simple stripes and bands set on a borderless fabric: thus was conceived the Chinle regional style.

Encouraged by the restoration of soft vegetal dye tones, but desiring a wider range of colors, those interested in Navajo weaving questioned the feasibility of creating such colors from commercial dyes. Miss Lucy C. Cabot, a dye expert in Boston, Massachusetts, was consulted and subsequently a series of tests was initiated with the DuPont Chemical Company. The result was a series of manufactured dyes in a highly concentrated form, using 28 percent acetic acid as a mordant to be mixed with a desired colorant. In 1932,

the dyes were introduced on the Reservation. The solutions resulted in beautiful yarns, and weavers were pleased by the flexibility of tones that could be achieved. In the months that followed, the Diamond Dye Company produced an improved series called *Old Navaho*. This product combined in one package the mordant with the colorant, thus relieving the weaver of hazardous procedures of acid mixings. Today, most Chinle regional style rugs reflect both the vegetal and commercial dye experiments of the Revival Period.

Further experimentation with native dye plants was undertaken in the late 1930's, by Mr. and Mrs. William Lippincott, of Wide Ruins Trading Post. They encouraged their weavers in the selection of subtle colors. Their labors met with excellent results, giving rise to a distinctive, well woven product called the Wide Ruins, which today denotes an all-vegetal colored rug.

The success of vegetal dyes did not end with the field tests at Chinle and Wide Ruins, but was carried on in laboratory experiments at Fort Wingate Vocational High School east of Gallup, New Mexico. Here two women, Nonabah G. Bryan and Stella Young, conducted six years of research on native plants. A combination resulting in 84 shades of color dyes. Findings of their study were published in 1940 under the title, *Navajo Native Dyes, Their Preparation and Use,* by the U.S. Department of The Interior. The recipe instruction type manual was widely circulated both on and off the Reservation, and for those weavers who desired to work with vegetal dye methods, the step-by-step procedures became an invaluable aid. In recent years, over 240 color tones have been achieved from native plant dyes, and the combinations from them are innumerable. This research and its application represents one of the greatest contributions in the history of Navajo weaving. The increased esthetic quality character of the dye products, in the eyes of the white man, will in all probability extend the life of the craft.

Two other significant events occurred before the close of the Revival Period. First, was establishment of the Navajo Sheep Breeding Laboratory at Fort Wingate in 1934. Directed by the U.S. Department of Agriculture, programs were initiated to improve the

Rambouillet strain, mainly through selective breeding with existing flocks. The success of the project provided a balance between high mutton production and finer grades of fleece. Secondly, came establishment of the Navajo Arts and Crafts Guild in 1941. This Window Rock based organization provided quality controls and protection for the weaver, as well as assistance in procurement of good weaving materials and fair market outlets.

Regional Style Period: 1940-Present

As previously outlined, four areas were beginning to emerge as style centers in preceding periods: the Moore-Crystal and Hubbell-Ganado during the Rug Period (1890-1920); and the McSparron-Chinle and Lippincott-Wide Ruins in the Revival Period (1920-1940). Early in the development of the Regional Style Period, weavers in other areas sought to create new designs, ideas and arrangements of patterns and color that would be commercially attractive. As indicated previously, those rugs whose history began with imaginative traders became the modern standard bearers of the Regional Style Period. Other areas at one time were considered style centers, but failed to develop distinction, or through merging of characteristics with stronger centers lost their identities.

Today, there are six additional style-type rugs associated with certain geographic locations on the Reservation. They are: Shiprock, Teec Nos Pos, Lukachukai, Two Gray Hills, the "new" Crystal, and the area designated as Western Reservation.[5] Each of these regional types is different, characterized by its own distinctive style, color, dye, and design that can be identified at a glance as to its weaving center. In recent years an element of pride has developed in these centers, to emphasize the individualism of style.

It is interesting to note that while the regional style rug is the dominant textile force in Navajoland at the present time, it accounts for only about 25 percent of total rug production. There is no law governing regional style weaving. Some weavers, regardless of their Reservation home, may prefer the vegetal dyes and designs of a Crystal while residing near Ganado. A few are classed as combination weavers. These rare artists, who usually live in the vicinity of two rug regions, can produce two styles of design of equal excellence. Not all weavers are geared to regional styles; the majority like to combine styles, experiment with dyes, color arrangements, and designs, and more or less create something entirely different from what is dictated by the region in which they live. The resultant pieces are called general rugs. Another type of weaver who does excellent work is the artist who undertakes to create a difficult specialty, such as the Two-Faced, Pictorial, Sandpainting, and Raised Outline product. In the better quality weaves, these rugs often command greater prices than the regional ones. Another often overlooked woven style is the Saddle Blanket. Hundreds of these less expensive, coarsely made, simply designed fabrics come off the Reservation annually. Demand for these pieces remains fairly constant, not only because they are functional as horse trappings but also as colorful, durable floor items.

The approximate breakdown of present rug production types on the Reservation is as follows:

General Rugs 40%
Saddle Blankets 30%
Regional Style Rugs 25%
Specialty Rugs 5%

Navajo rugs produced during the Regional Style Period represent the craft at its peak of artistic expression and acceptance, although cost and demand have spiraled prices above reach of the average buyer. Versatility and quality are high, with some experts claiming finer craftsmanship, color balance, and design than at any time in the 250 year history of Navajo weaving.

From inception of the Regional Style Period the numbers of rugs have gradually decreased. Prices began to soar in the early 1960's, with the current annual increase in Navajo rug prices at about 20%. Buyers are demanding quality, and only the talented craftswoman can realize the full worth of her product. It is apparent that Navajo rugs are becoming fewer and fewer, with many prize fabrics falling into the hands of collectors.

The craft today is not economically attractive for the average weaver. Younger women are not following in their mothers' avocations. Many are becoming more educated and leaving the Reservation for more lucrative jobs. In the Crystal and Lukachukai areas alone there are only five name weavers remaining. A renaissance of sorts is under way, however; resurgence of interest in Indian arts and crafts is occurring, and weaving classes are now being offered. On the Reservation some new life is being instilled in the craft, although it remains to be seen what trends and directions Navajo weaving will embark upon during its 100th anniversary era since Bosque Redondo.

In summary, history has dealt kindly with the craft. Surviving two severe depressions and, with borrowed necessities like the Pueblo loom, Spanish and French sheep, German and English yarn, and American yarns and dyes, it has managed surprisingly well. The rug came into being because the white man accepted a textile that satisfied his esthetic needs at a particular time, and because of it, the white man has come to a better understanding of the red man.

The Navajo's love of beauty is reflected in the rug and perhaps the verse of the Navajo Ceremony, the *Night Way*, best summarizes the spirit of their lives:

> *In beauty, I shall walk.*
> *In beauty, you shall be my picture.*
> *In beauty, you shall be my song.*
> *In beauty, you shall be my medicine.*
> *In beauty, my holy medicine.*[6]

Chapter 2

From Sheep to Rug

THE SHEEP: The Navajo people, particularly the women, lead a pastoral existence. They are "sheep-minded"; from sunup to sundown, their main concern is for their flocks. The herding life is strenuous, especially in winter months when freezing snows blanket the sparse grasslands, forcing herds into constant wanderings in search of food.

The "Navajo sheep" is not a particular breed. The principal flocks raised on the Reservation are a mixture of various strains, including the French Rambouillet strains of the Merino breed supplemented with Corriedale rams. The main ancestral line is probably still the old Spanish churro. The fleece is relatively heavy, yielding approximately 8-10 pounds per animal.

SHEARING: The first step in conversion of wool to rug is shearing, usually accomplished in early spring when the fleece has attained its greatest thickness. Small portions of the flock are corralled at a time, whereupon the shearer will sweep a sand-cleared spot on the ground and commence with the flanking and ultimate shearing of the animal. Ordinarily metal shears are used. There is no system to the operation, although a skillful worker will clip from the neck toward the tail,

making efforts to keep the fleece in one piece. The select wool is obtained from the back, at the shoulders, and along the flanks. The remaining shorter fibers are separated and bagged for sale at the trading post.

CLEANING: Shorn wool, earmarked for weaving, is then hand cleaned of burrs, sticks and other debris. A fluffing technique accompanies the general cleaning and the wool is laid out for a short period for airing and drying of animal oils. Some weavers sprinkle white clay or pulverized selenite (gypsum) on the fleece to absorb oil and dirt which is carried in the oil. If the shorn wool is exceptionally dirty, a wet washing may then be necessary to remove saturated impurities.

CARDING: The purpose of carding is to straighten the tangled fibers into loose, uniform pads. Small handfuls of the washed wool are hand-fluffed and then raked across two hand-held, metal-toothed towcards. This technique combs the wool into slender fibers that can be easily spun. Carding also serves as a second cleaning. Persistent friction of the forward and backward towing removes most remaining particles of grit. Carding is the least enjoyable task in the rug process. It requires considerable strength in the

The Sheep

Shearing

hands and arms in an unnatural cramped position. Recently, more weavers are turning to machine-carded (processed wool) skeins of yarn, usually commercially dyed, which can be purchased at trading posts.

SPINNING: This process accounts for the type of yarn that will determine the strength and weight of the rug. The Navajo technique of spinning remains as traditional as the craft itself. No machine procedure is involved. Instead, a simple spindle stick and whorl, about 12" long, resembling a miniature ski pole, is manipulated with the hands. The base of the spindle is seated on the ground with the shaft twirled on the thigh with the right hand while the left regulates thickness of the fiber. Two spinnings are usually required to produce weft yarns. Additional respinnings will produce finer and finer threads, thus resulting in a more finely woven rug. If a weaver chooses, she can bypass the spinning step and purchase commercial prespun yarn, usually in a wide range of colors, over the trading post counter.

WASHING: Before the yarn is dyed, it is necessary that it be washed. The only soap the early Navajos knew, and which is still preferred by many, was the high lathers, obtained from roots of the broad-leaved yucca, mainly *Yucca baccata* in central Navajo country, and the narrow leaved yuccas, such as *Yucca glauca* and *Yucca standleyi*. Both agents can be used fresh or dried and may be gathered at any season of the year. The broad leaved yucca is the stronger and more desirable of the two. After a thorough washing, including at least two rinses, care is taken not to squeeze, twist, or wring out the wool, as it promotes lumping and knotting of the fibers. Instead, the wool should be floated freely in the water and removed carefully and placed on boards, rocks, etc. for sun-drying.

DYEING: Various degrees of color can be achieved by the modern weaver. In some cases, a combination will prevail in a single rug. In the natural wool tones,

such as utilized at Two Gray Hills, shades of tan, beige, and gray can be attained in the carding step by blending desired amounts of black, brown, and white wools.[7] In other instances, bright commercial anilines purchased over the counter can be used in addition to vegetal-dyed wools. If a weaver wishes to dye her own yarn, it is done after the spinning and washing.

Vegetal-dyed techniques require considerable more time and effort for preparation of the yarn. In the publication, *Navajo Native Dyes*, Nonabah G. Bryan and Stella Young outline the following procedures for the dyeing of one color. *"She selects an enamel kettle for dyeing, because she found that if she does it in tin or aluminum the acid developed in the dyebath while fermenting reacts upon the metal, and the color of the dye is changed. She measures out the dried prickly pear fruit and covers it with lukewarm water to soak overnight. In the morning she mashes it well, strains it, and adds enough more cool water to cover the yarn completely. She then places the wet yarn in it, rubs the dye into it well, covers it, and sets it in a warm place to ferment, having learned from previous experience that if she boils it the lovely rose color will change to tan. Many times each day during the following week she rubs the dye into the yarn. If she finds at the end of the time that the rose color is not as deep as she wishes it, she puts it in another dyebath of the same strength as before and allows it to ferment another week. She then rinses it thoroughly and hangs it up to dry.*[8] The authors, Bryan and Young, follow with a list of ten basic observations that should be heeded in the vegetal dyeing of rugs.

1. *The same species of plant grown in different sections of the country may give different shades of color. The shade of color may also vary from year to year from a plant grown in the same locality.*

2. *All dye plants may be used with or without a mordant. The use of a mordant deepens the color and occasionally changes it.*

15

Cleaning

Carding

16

The use of a different mordant, or varying the quantity of mordant used, also produces a difference in the color given by the same plant. Colors dyed without a mordant are reasonably fast.

3. *Longer boiling of the dye with the yarn usually produces a deeper color. Occasionally the color is entirely changed.*

4. *Allowing the yarn to remain in the dyebath overnight deepens and brightens the color. It is believed that it also produces a faster color.*

Spinning

5. *It is necessary that most of the dyes be boiled with the yarn to produce the color. There are exceptions to this, however. Cactus fruit, some berries and flowers lose their color when boiled. For this reason we allow the dye to ferment into the yarn as explained in the recipes.*

6. *The afterbath yarn, or the second yarn dyed in the same dyewater, is a softer, lighter tint of the same color.*

Dyeing

7. *Most of the plants may be used either fresh or dried. Fresh plants are usually stronger than when dried. Therefore, less of the fresh is required to produce the same color. Dried canaigre root, however, is stronger than when it is fresh. One must bear this in mind when substituting in the following recipes.*

8. *Dried barks, plants, and fruits should be soaked overnight before using.*

9. *Yarns must be rinsed several times after dyeing to remove the unabsorbed dye.*

10. *The yarns dyed by the following recipes have been tested for color fastness when treated with commercial cleaners and moth preventives and were found to be unchanged by them.* [9]

In arriving at colors in vegetal dyeing, the yellows are the easiest to obtain and range from clear yellow through greenish-yellows to mustard to gold. The browns have a range from beige to dark colored browns to deep rose and tan-reds. The most frequently found colors are orange, gray, tan, coral, brown, yellow, and variable tints of rose. A good solid green is hard to obtain and additional color baths, such as yellow mixed with blue, are usually required. Listed below are the 84 basic sources and colors listed in *Navajo Native Dyes.* This is by no means the complete color range of vegetal dyes. The shades, tints, hues, and combinations of plant colors reach infinity. The following examples form the basis of plant usage now generally in practice on the Reservation. In several instances, one plant can produce several hues of color. This can be accomplished by controlling the strength of the dyebath (cooking time) and varying the recipe (amount of vegetal matter used).

PARTIAL LIST OF VEGETAL DYE COLORS AND SOURCES

Color #1	Light Greenish-Yellow	Actinea Flower, Multiple-Flowered (Flowers and Leaves)
Color #2	Yellow	Actinea Flower, Single-Flowered (Flowers and Leaves)
Color #3	Soft Brown	Alder Tree (Bark)
Color #4	Tan-Beige	Alder Tree (Bark)
Color #5	Yellow-Green	Beeplant (Leaves)
Color #6	Greenish-Yellow	Bitterball (Leaves)
Color #7	Pale Greenish-Yellow	Bitterball (Leaves)
Color #8	Mustard	Bitterball (Leaves)
Color #9	Rose	Prickly Pear Cactus
Color #10	Deep Rose	Prickly Pear Cactus
Color #11	Light Rose	Prickly Pear Cactus
Color #12	Pink with a Light Tan	Prickly Pear Cactus
Color #13	Tan	Prickly Pear Cactus
Color #14	Coral Pink	Prickly Pear Cactus and Mountain Mahogany (Root Bark)

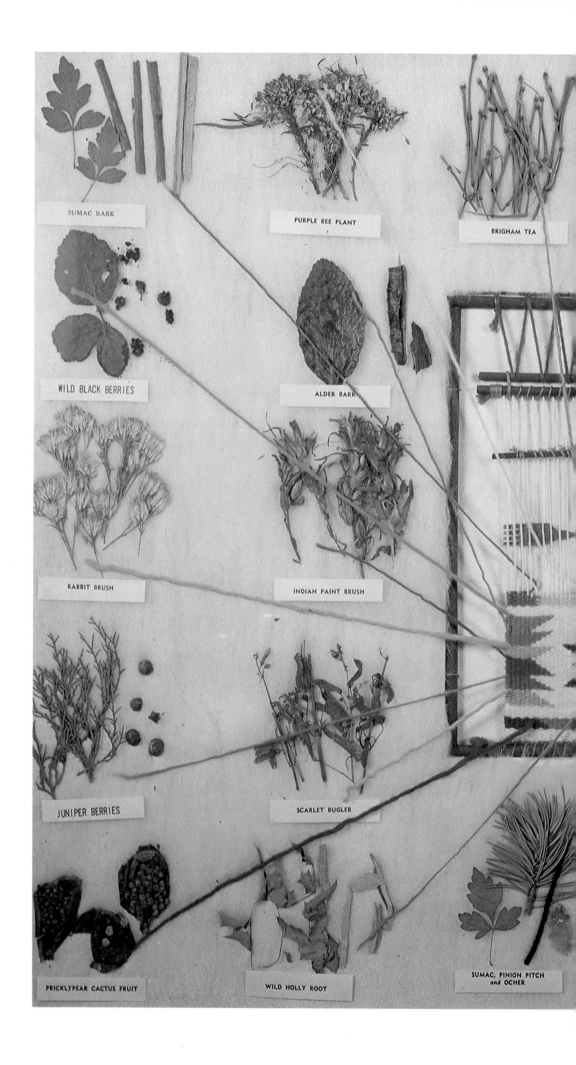

SUMAC BARK

PURPLE BEE PLANT

BRIGHAM TEA

WILD BLACK BERRIES

ALDER BARK

RABBIT BRUSH

INDIAN PAINT BRUSH

JUNIPER BERRIES

SCARLET BUGLER

PRICKLYPEAR CACTUS FRUIT

WILD HOLLY ROOT

SUMAC, PINION PITCH and OCHER

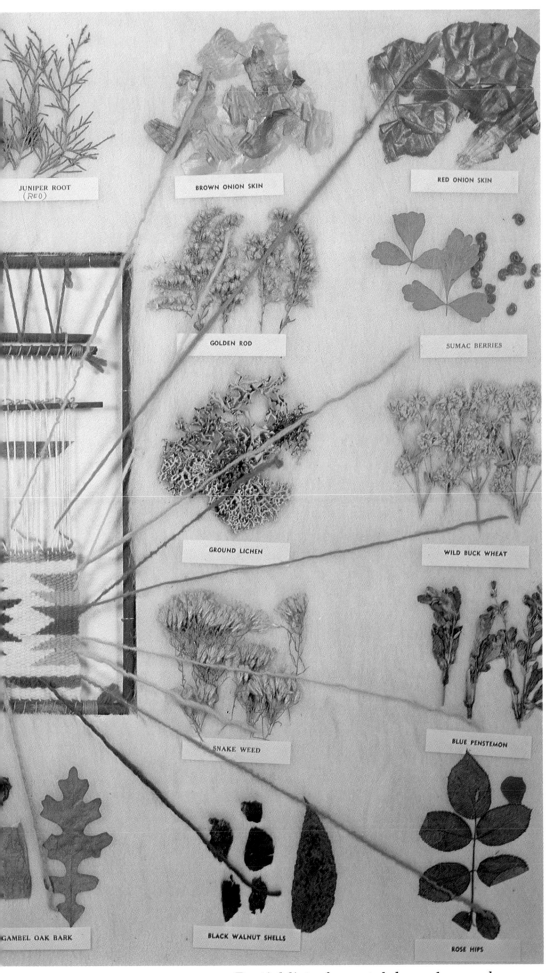

JUNIPER ROOT
(RED)

BROWN ONION SKIN

RED ONION SKIN

GOLDEN ROD

SUMAC BERRIES

GROUND LICHEN

WILD BUCK WHEAT

SNAKE WEED

BLUE PENSTEMON

GAMBEL OAK BARK

BLACK WALNUT SHELLS

ROSE HIPS

Partial list of vegetal-dye colors and sources

Color #15	Medium Brown	Canaigre (Roots)
Color #16	Yellow-Orange	Canaigre (Roots)
Color #17	Light Canary Yellow	Wild Celery (Flowers)
Color #18	Bright Yellow	Chamizo (Leaves, Twigs and Blossoms)
Color #19	Light Canary Yellow	Chamizo (Leaves, Twigs and Blossoms)
Color #20	Mustard	Chamizo (Leaves, Twigs and Blossoms)
Color #21	Purplish-Brown	Chokecherry (Root Bark) and Wild Plum (Root Bark)
Color #22	Bright Yellow	Owls' Claws (Leaves, Twigs and Blossoms)
Color #23	Light Canary Yellow	Owls' Claws (Leaves, Twigs and Blossoms)
Color #24	Mustard	Owls' Claws (Leaves, Twigs and Blossoms)
Color #25	Dulled Greenish-Yellow	Oregon Grape (Roots, Leaves and Stems)
Color #26	Light Gray	Ironwood (Berries)
Color #27	Orange-Tan	One-Seeded Juniper (Twigs)
Color #28	Yellow-Tan	One-Seeded Juniper (Twigs)
Color #29	Greenish-Gray	Wild Purple Larkspur (Petals)
Color #30	Light Greenish-Yellow	Wild Purple Larkspur (Flowers, Leaves and Stems)
Color #31	Light Orange	Ground Lichen
Color #32	Reddish-Tan	Ground Lichen
Color #33	Yellow-Tan	Ground Lichen
Color #34	Greenish-Yellow	Blue-Flowered Lupine (Flowers, Leaves and Stems)
Color #35	Soft Reddish-Brown	Mountain Mahogany (Root Bark)
Color #36	Deep Reddish-Brown	Mountain Mahogany (Root Bark) with Juniper Ashes
Color #37	Rose Taupe	Mountain Mahogany (Root Bark) with Cactus Fruit
Color #38	Soft Reddish-Tan	Mountain Mahogany (Root Bark) with Cactus Fruit
Color #39	Dark Burnt Orange	Mountain Mahogany (Root Bark) with Navajo Tea
Color #40	Henna	Mountain Mahogany (Root Bark) with Navajo Tea
Color #41	Light Red-Brown	Mountain Mahogany (Root Bark) with Ground Lichens
Color #42	Light Brown	Mountain Mahogany (Root Bark) with Alder Bark
Color #43	Reddish-Tan	Mountain Mahogany (Root Bark) with Alder Bark
Color #44	Soft Cream Tan	Mountain Mahogany (Root Bark) with Alder Bark
Color #45	Light Brown	Mountain Mahogany (Root Bark) with Alder Bark
Color #46	Dulled Tan	Gambel Oak (Bark)
Color #47	Light Gold	Scrub Oak (Gall)
Color #48	Light Yellowish-Tan	Scrub Oak (Gall)
Color #49	Tan	Indian Paintbrush (Blossoms)
Color #50	Greenish-Yellow	Indian Paintbrush (Leaves, Stems and Blossoms)
Color #51	Dull Tan	Pinedrop (Entire Plant)
Color #52	Reddish-Purple	Wild Plum (Roots)
Color #53	Bright Yellow	Rabbitbrush, Large (Blossoms and Twigs)
Color #54	Light Canary Yellow	Rabbitbrush, Large (Blossoms and Twigs)
Color #55	Mustard	Rabbitbrush, Large (Blossoms and Twigs)
Color #56	Bright Yellow	Rabbitbrush, Small (Blossoms and Twigs)
Color #57	Light Canary Yellow	Rabbitbrush, Small (Blossoms and Twigs)
Color #58	Mustard	Rabbitbrush, Small (Blossoms and Twigs)
Color #59	Gold	Cliff Rose (Twigs and Leaves)
Color #60	Bright Yellow	Rubberplant (Leaves, Stems and Flowers)
Color #61	Light Canary Yellow	Rubberplant (Leaves, Stems and Flowers)
Color #62	Mustard	Rubberplant (Leaves, Stems and Flowers)
Color #63	Slight Greenish-Yellow	Basin Sagebrush (Leaves and Twigs)
Color #64	Pale Greenish-Yellow	Basin Sagebrush (Leaves and Twigs)
Color #65	Mustard	Basin Sagebrush (Leaves and Twigs)
Color #66	Gold	Basin Sagebrush (Leaves and Twigs)

Color #67	Rich Olive Green	Basin Sagebrush (Leaves and Twigs)
Color #68	Medium Olive Green	Basin Sagebrush (Leaves and Twigs)
Color #69	Bluish-Black	Sumac (Leaves), Piñon Pitch, Yellow Ocher
Color #70	Light Oxford Gray	Sumac (Leaves), Piñon Pitch, Yellow Ocher
Color #71	Light Orange Brown	Sumac (Berries)
Color #72	Light Tan	Mormon Tea (Twigs and Leaves)
Color #73	Orange	Navajo Tea (Flowers)
Color #74	Light Orange	Navajo Tea (Flowers)
Color #75	Light Olive Green	Navajo Tea (Leaves)
Color #76	Orange	Navajo Tea (Leaves and Flowers) and Canaigre (Root)
Color #77	Pineneedle Green	Navajo Tea (Leaves) and Black Dyewater
Color #78	Dull Olive Green	Russian Thistle (Entire Plant)
Color #79	Deep Tan	Russian Thistle (Young Plant)
Color #80	Rich Brown	Wild Walnut Hulls
Color #81	Gray Tan	Wild Walnut Hulls
Color #82	Rich Tan	Wild Walnut Hulls
Color #83	Light Tan	Wild Walnut (Leaves)
Color #84	Salmon Pink	Brick-colored rainwater from red mesas in Arizona and New Mexico [10]

THE LOOM: The Navajo loom consists of two uprights and two crosspieces of log-size wood 6″ to 8″ in diameter, usually cut from piñon trees. The lower crosspiece, serving as the base, must be composed of the heaviest wood to support the balance of the frame. Legs of wood may be constructed at right angles to the uprights to serve as additional supports. It is very important that the entire structure be rigid.

WARPING THE LOOM: When the weaver has determined the size of rug she wishes to weave, the warp thread is prepared. [11] The warp thread, or strand, serves as the foundation of the rug. It is necessarily stronger to support the total body of woven wefts. The stringing of the warp is done on a warpframe, a temporary device separated from the loom proper, consisting of two long boards forming the sides and two securely tied crosspieces (usually of 1″ dowel or broomstick size) at each end. The warpframe is laid horizontally on the ground, elevated a few inches by rocks at the four corners. If there is sufficient room inside the warpframe (considering the size of the proposed rug), the weaver can position herself within the enclosure and commence the stringing.

The warp is one continuous strand that is wound in a figure-eight pattern at approximately 1/4″ intervals around the two dowel crosspieces. Constant tension of the warp is maintained as the strand is passed over the dowel on the outside and returned under the dowel on the inside, thus creating warp-pairs. The two figure eight patterns created are called sheds, established by the insertion and tieing of two sticks, called shed rods, into the warp pattern. During actual weaving, manipulation of the shed rods creates the needed spaces for passing of the weft threads.

To secure their equally spaced position on the dowel, the

Warping The Loom

warp is then edged off by a twining cord to form a stabilizing top and bottom border.

When the entire warp is strung and secured, the warpframe is dismantled and the warp is transferred and mounted on the permanent upright loom by lashing the warp dowels, now referred to as the warp beam (upper) and the web beam (lower), with a lightweight rope. The warp beam is actually attached to another dowel, called the stick, that can be rope lowered or raised to desired heights. The shed rods are then untied, but not removed. The warp is straightened within the loom frame and a desired tension is applied to make the entire harness a taut unit.

WEAVING: The basic Navajo weave is the tapestry technique in which the warp threads are usually completely concealed by passage of the weft yarn.[12] To facilitate passing of the wefts through the warp lines, shed rods are employed. The upper shed rod is a loosely inserted stick placed between alternating warps. The lower shed rod (sometimes called a heddle rod), is secured to opposite alternating warp threads. By manipulating shed rod and heddle, odd numbered warps can be brought forward and separated from even numbered warps. To enlarge the opening for weaving, a flat stick called a batten (18″ to 24″ long, 1″ wide) is inserted and turned on edge. The wefts ultimately are tamped into place by a wooden toothed comb called the fork.

The designs that originate in a rug generally evolve in the imagination of the weaver before she begins to weave. Traditional Navajo designs usually are handed down from one generation to another. As a result, a repetition of colors and basic motifs can prevail in a weaving family.

According to Bill Young, trader at Hubbell Trading Post, a good to average weaver can accomplish approximately one square foot of weave per day. [13]

When the rug is completed, the weaver offers the result for sale at the trading post. Recognizing the value and time that she spent on the rug, she will understandably negotiate for the best price possible. If necessary, she will try several neighboring posts until satisfaction is met. During earlier times when travel was somewhat restricted on the Reservation, rugs were sold in proximity to the weaver's home. Today, with the ubiquitous pickup truck speeding along improved highways, the weaver may travel a hundred miles or more to get her asking price. Considering this "roaming about" of rugs, it may be confusing at times to see a regional style weave such as a Two Gray Hills on the rack at Hubbell Trading Post, and vice versa. For this reason then, many Reservation outlets now stock a good selection of representative rug types. If a purchaser is not aware of identifying characteristics, it is easy to be misled. One of the most common mistakes made in regional style names is to label a rug by the trading post from which it was purchased.

The Loom

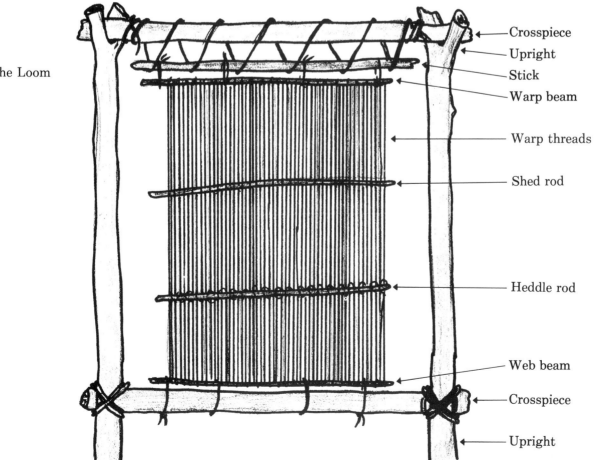

Crosspiece
Upright
Stick
Warp beam

Warp threads

Shed rod

Heddle rod

Web beam

Crosspiece

Upright

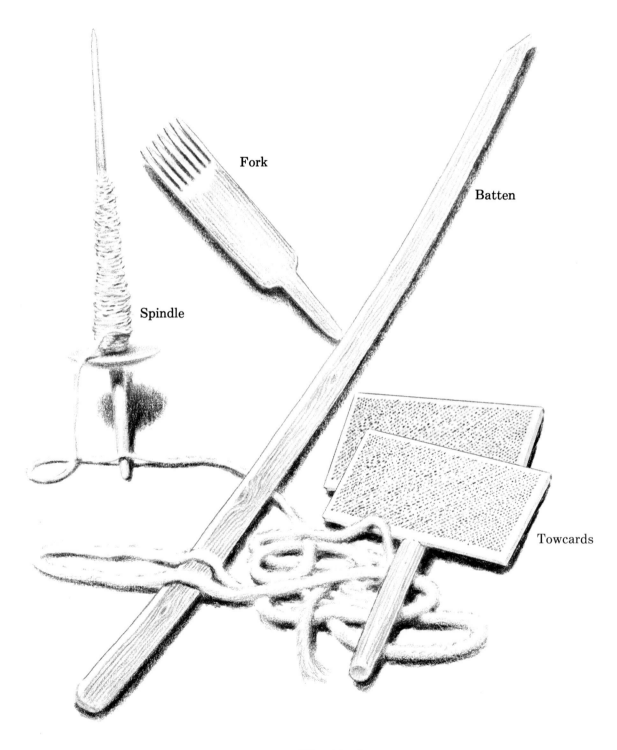

Fork

Batten

Spindle

Towcards

The Tools

Weaving

Selling to the Trader

TIME-COST RUG CHART
(SHEEP TO RUG)

EXAMPLE: 3 x 5 vegetal-dyed rug (high quality)

Activity	Hours
Shearing (2 sheep)	2
Cleaning	10
Carding	40
Spinning	90
Washing	8
Native plant gatherings (5 colors)	4
Dyeing	40
Loom Construction	16
Warping the loom	18
Weaving	160
TOTAL	388 hours (48.5 days)
Probable Sale	$500.00
Average	1.30 per hour

It is understandable that at an average of $1.30 per hour (and many are woven for a lot less), the weaving of a Navajo rug is hard work for the money. The cost is justified. The current price varies considerably from one rug style to another.

Considering those fabrics that are well woven, the fine anilines are running from $50 to $100 a square foot; vegetal dyes $100 to $150 a square foot; and the natural wool products of a Two Gray Hills, upwards of $200 a square foot.

(Above figures compiled with the assistance of Mr. John Rieffer of Wide Ruins Trading Post, August, 1973).

Shiprock Trading Company — and the ever present, ubiquitous pickup truck.

Chapter 3

Shiprock

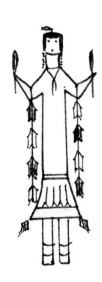

Elevation: 4903′
Post Office Established: 1904
Owner-Trader: Ed Foutz

THE POST

The town of Shiprock is located on the San Juan River in extreme northwestern New Mexico.[14] Its present name is derived from a volcanic neck called Shiprock, a towering igneous mass that dominates the landscape ten miles southwest of the town. In Navajo mythology the majestic rock is called *Tse Bit'a'i,* meaning "rock with wings," or "winged rock."

Origin of the Shiprock site dates from 1872 when Thomas Keam scouted the area for the U.S. Government for location of a Fort Defiance sub-agency office. Plans for construction of the agency did not materialize until September 11, 1903. The first buildings were built of logs and adobe, replaced by brick structures after the disastrous flood of 1911.

The first superintendent of the Shiprock Agency was W. T. Shelton, a man whose contribution to Navajo weaving has been largely overlooked in contemporary writings. In 1909, Shelton conceived the idea of holding Navajo fairs, inviting not only Indians, but traders as well, to display their extensive exhibits of Navajo craftsmanship. The Shiprock conclaves, held annually the first week of October, were a great success. The principal theme was the presentation of rugs and silversmithing for which prizes were awarded.

Rug displays at Shiprock Fair, circa 1912.

These rare and informative photographs illustrate many important facts.

Bottom: The examples on the right, under the Two Gray Hills John-Davies banner, exhibit typical Crystal characteristics, thus establishing John B. Moore's contribution in the development of the early Two Gray Hills rug. The multiple geometrics of the modern-day Two Gray Hills did not emerge until the mid 1920's. Note the Storm Pattern elements in the rug beneath the Reitz name. To the left are rugs from the Shiprock area; the Yeis had not yet made their appearance by 1912. Most of the examples reflect Teec Nos Pos designs.

Top: Newly, brick-constructed Shiprock Agency buildings backdrop the fair displays. Chimney smoke and smoldering bonfire ashes (both photos) suggest a brisk early fall morning. Unexplained erroneous spelling of Teec Nos Pos ("EastNos-Pos") to the right.

(Photo courtesy: Gilbert Maxwell and Best-West Publications).

In the 1912 fair over 400 pieces of weaving were displayed. Publicity received for the Indian through the Shiprock fairs proved an invaluable asset.

The first trading post in the area was operated as Robert Baker's Shiprock Trading Post. Bruce Bernard bought the Baker property in 1909 and ran it until his death in 1952. Another post, operated by the partnership of Walker and Hubbard, was purchased in 1912 by Will Evans. The Evans store was purchased by the Jack's Brothers in the summer of 1948, who in turn sold out to Russell Foutz in 1954. The holdings were recently transferred to a nephew, Ed Foutz, in late 1972, who operates the post as the Shiprock Trading Company.

THE RUG

The Shiprock rug type is called a Yei (pronounced "yea"). It was developed by Will Evans around the World War I period from stylized sandpaintings.[15] The Yei is a colorful piece that depicts religious figures but has no religious significance. The rug is usually of small to moderate size carrying bright colored, slender, front-facing figures surrounded by, in most cases, a red and blue figured rainbow goddess that serves as a border down the sides and across the bottom. Additional designs usually include interspacings of cornstalks and arrows. Backgrounds are usually white or light tan, with lesser amounts of dark and light blends of gray. The rug is finely-woven with a growing use of more commercial yarn. The Yei usually lends itself as a wall hanging in the same manner as a fine painting.

Another type of rug woven in the Shiprock area is the Yeibechai. Similar in size, gay colors, and commercial yarn to the Yei, the Yeibechai is a bordered rug (sometimes incorporating a design), that illustrates Navajo dancers, usually in profile, impersonating the Yei figures.

Shiprock Yei

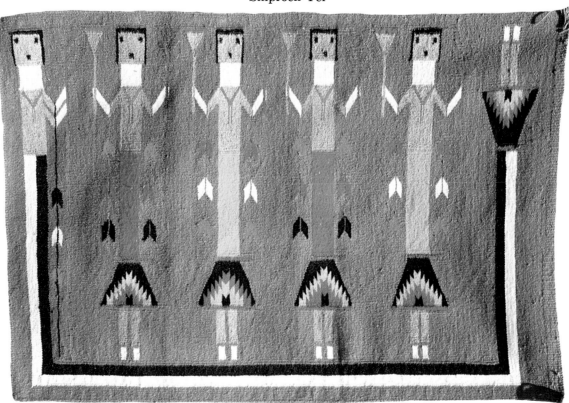

Shiprock Yei

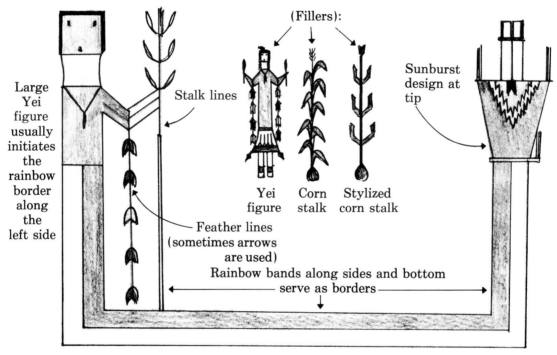

Large Yei figure usually initiates the rainbow border along the left side

Stalk lines

(Fillers):

Yei figure

Corn stalk

Stylized corn stalk

Sunburst design at tip

Feather lines (sometimes arrows are used)

Rainbow bands along sides and bottom serve as borders

Shiprock Yei Designs

Shiprock Yeibechai

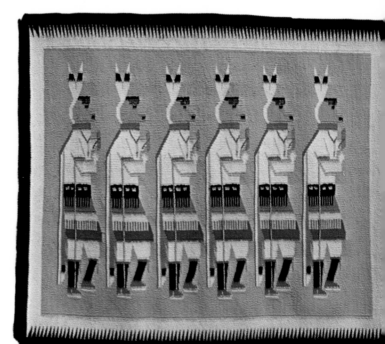

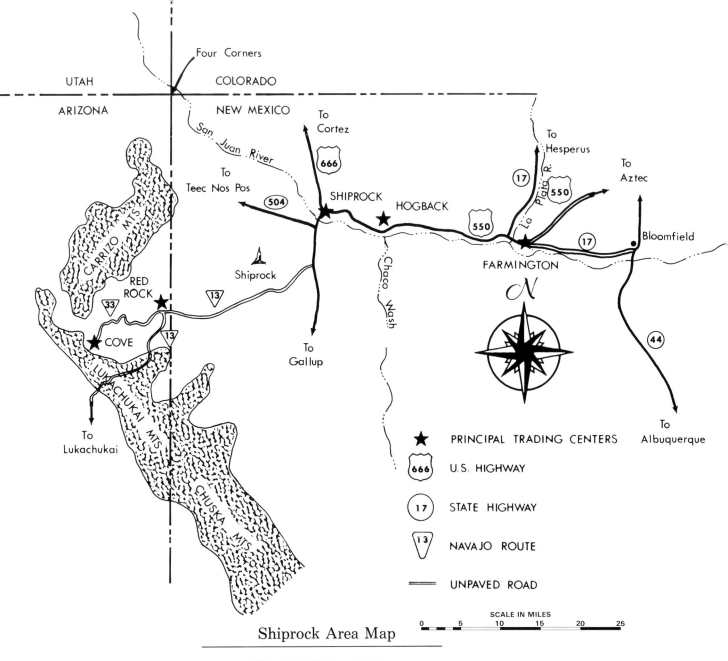

Shiprock Area Map

WEAVING AREA

Trading Posts

Bernard Trading Post (Shiprock)
Cove Trading Post
Russell Foutz Indian Room (Farmington)
Hogback Trading Post
Red Rock Trading Post (Pop. 2,253)
Shiprock Trading Company (Pop. 6,561)

Traders

Bruce Bernard
Raymond Ismay
Russell Foutz
Lloyd Wheeler
Troy Kennedy
Ed Foutz

WEAVERS

Daisy Barton   Lucy Farley
Lucy Chase   Mary Long (combination Yei and Teec Nos Pos weaver)
Pricilla Ectilly   Lola Yazzie (combination Yei and Teec Nos Pos weaver)

COMPARATIVE COSTS
(Range: $15-1$100 per Square Foot)

Year	3 x 5
1964	$ 50-$300
1974	$150-$600

35

The road to Lukachukai.

Chapter 4

Lukachukai

"White patch of reeds extends out"

Elevation: 9460′
Post Office
Established:
1916
Owner-Trader:
Kenneth
Kennedy

THE POST

Lukachukai is pronounced "look-a-choo-ki." The settlement is located along the west base of a tremendous red-rock escarpment of the Lukachukai Mountains. The immediate area is one of the most scenic on the Reservation. Transition from a sage-covered plain to forests and meadows is quite abrupt, leading some writers to refer to the highlands as the "Navajo Alps." The Indians call the mountains *Shiink'eh,* or "summer place."

The first trading post was established in 1892 by George N. Barker, at a site approximately one and a half miles east of the present location. George Washington Sampson, a veteran trader who managed a chain of trading posts, operated the store for a time following the turn of the century. Some references include the name Rico Menapase as being an active trader in the area, but no firm dates have been found to bracket his activities; possibly he occupied a brief time slot between Sampson and W. R. Cassidy. A license transfer shows that Cassidy sold out to Earl Kennedy in October, 1928.[16] Earl's son, Kenneth, assumed managership of the store following his father's death in September, 1971.

37

THE RUG

The Lukachukai area is a second source of the Yei rug. Here the products are of larger size, representing a greater use of handspun yarn, and the use of aniline dyes for color. Backgrounds are usually gray, red, black, or brown colored. In some examples the rug may be bordered outside of the rainbow goddess, usually in a dark color. In many pieces, the rainbow goddess is completely eliminated, with a solitary heavy border enclosing the figures. More figures occupy the Lukachukai Yei, but are less detailed and colorful. Also, the Yei figures tend to take on a more human appearance, similar to the front-facing Yeibechais. The basic motif is the same as in the rugs along the San Juan River, but as those to the northeast are suitable for the wall, the heavier, coarse-textured Yeis from across the intervening mountains are more adaptable as a floor covering.

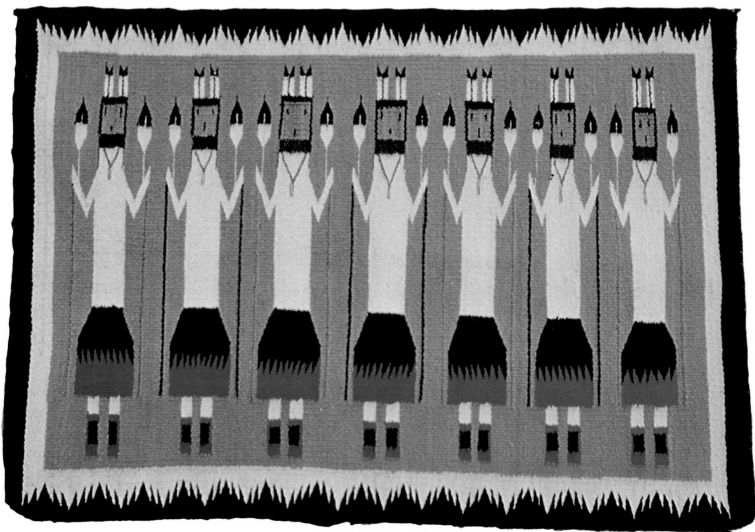

Plate 4. Lukachukai Yei

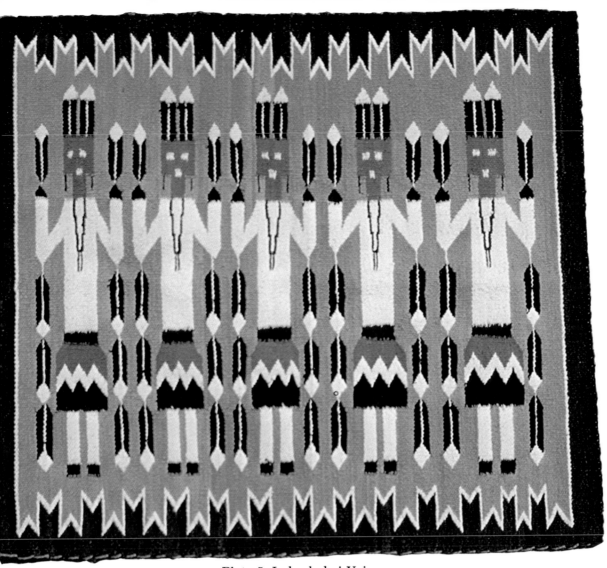

Plate 5. Lukachukai Yei

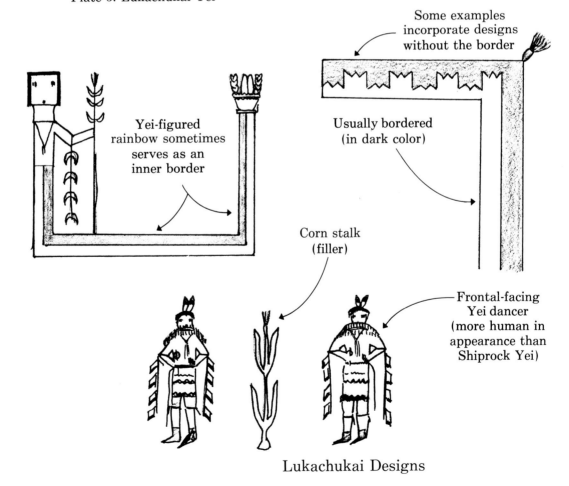

Some examples
incorporate designs
without the border

Yei-figured
rainbow sometimes
serves as an
inner border

Usually bordered
(in dark color)

Corn stalk
(filler)

Frontal-facing
Yei dancer
(more human in
appearance than
Shiprock Yei)

Lukachukai Designs

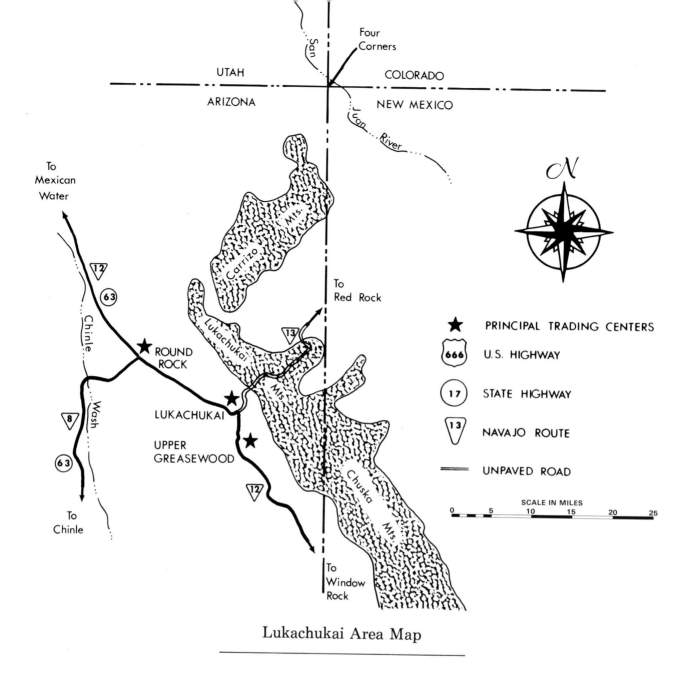

Lukachukai Area Map

WEAVING AREA

Trading Posts

Lukachukai Trading Post (Pop. 1,303)
Round Rock Trading Post (Pop. 1,055)
Totso Trading Post (Lukachukai)
Upper Greasewood Trading Post

Traders

Kenneth Kennedy
Raymond Blair
Alvin Jack — Dean Winn
C. E. Wheeler

WEAVERS

Mary Bahe   Annie Brady
Lucy Betony   Genevieve Brady
Rita Bitani

COMPARATIVE COSTS
(Range: $10 - $60 per square foot)

Year	3 x 5	4 x 6	6 x 9
1964	$50-125	$150-200	$300-500
1974	$75-200	$200-350	$600-1500

Teec Nos Pos — gateway to the Four Corners.

Chapter 5

Teec Nos Pos

"Circle of Cottonwoods"

Elevation: 5450'
Post Office Established: 1961
Trader: Bob French
Owner: Russell Foutz

THE POST

H. B. (Hambleton Bridger) Noel was not a timid soul. He established his Teec Nos Pos Trading Post in 1905 in the remote area west of Shiprock, with full knowledge that predecessors had been chased out. He bought a high powered automatic loading Remington rifle from a drummer, and made a point of going out with Navajos to shoot at rabbits or other targets. When satisfied that his prowess with a rifle was established, he hung the gun conspicuously on the wall back of the counter, in easy reach.

The improbable location that Noel chose was in foothills of the northern Carrizos, at the head of a cottonwood-lined canyon on Tisnosbas Creek. Furthermore, the bravery of the man led him into a region controlled by Black Horse, a clan chieftan whose dislike for the white man was displayed ten years earlier when he cleared the area of invading merchants. Before a single spadefull of dirt was turned, Noel was subjected to a trial of

41

several hundred Navajos who gathered at the canyon site to debate whether they should let this man with the corn colored hair from Essex County, Virginia, live among them. After a day-long council, the Indians voted to let him stay, for the region was distant and it seemed the time was right to link themselves to an outside source for marketing.

Noel traded at Teec Nos Pos for eight years, selling out to the partnership of Bert Dustin and Al Foutz and retiring to a farm at Fruitland, New Mexico. Russell Foutz of Fruit-land purchased the store in 1945. The old post was destroyed by fire in 1959. It was rebuilt the same year on a higher shelf of land a few miles to the north and east of its original location. Today, Teec Nos Pos has achieved a community atmosphere, and is a busy trading crossroads mainly because its strategic location serves as a gateway to the Four Corners Monument. Unfortunately, the place name site description of a "circle of cotton-woods" of the original canyon setting does not characterize the post's present location.

Noel's original Teec Nos Pos Trading Post, circa 1949. (Jack Snow photo, from M. Burge Collection, Photograph Collection, Museum of New Mexico).

Plate 6. Teec Nos Pos

THE RUG

The dedicated weavers of Teec Nos Pos produce a tightly woven rug that has been described by many as the "least Navajo" of all the regional styles. The rug has a Persian flair, probably devised by an early trader who circulated examples of this style among the area craftswomen. Trader Noel took no credit for the design, and according to Maxwell, was convinced that a Mrs. Wilson, a San Juan missionary, was responsible for influencing the weavers in this style. [17]

The Teec Nos Pos rug is very busy and intricate in design. Colors, often used in small amounts, are rather flamboyant. Bright greens, blue, orange, and reds are popular. Commercial yarns are more often used, with some utilization of aniline-dyed, handspun fibers. The typical Teec Nos Pos possesses a broad border that contains a design, usually a broad H, T, or L blocking. The rug primarily features a contrasting color outline of the main patterns which usually consist of zigzags, serrated diamonds, triangles, and boxes. Because of its usually bright, multiple colors, the Teec Nos Pos is more difficult to blend into home decorating schemes. It is therefore more popular as a collector's item.

Fifteen miles west of Teec Nos Pos lies the high, lonesome post of Red Mesa. Here a small group of weavers are producing the Teec Nos Pos outline designs in traditional handspun yarns of grays, white, black, maroons and dark red. Some writers have recognized the Red Mesa rug as a distinct regional style because of the local weavers' dislike for bright colors. The design, however, despite the subdued tones, remains typical Teec Nos Pos.

Plate 7. Teec Nos Pos

Slash panels

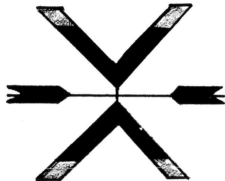

Outlined squash blossom

Plate 8. Teec Nos Pos

Combination half-diamonds
and arrow tips

Dominant center panel
of complex workings
of diamonds and various
outlined forms

Teec Nos Pos Designs

Lightning design

Bold heavy border
(usually dark color)

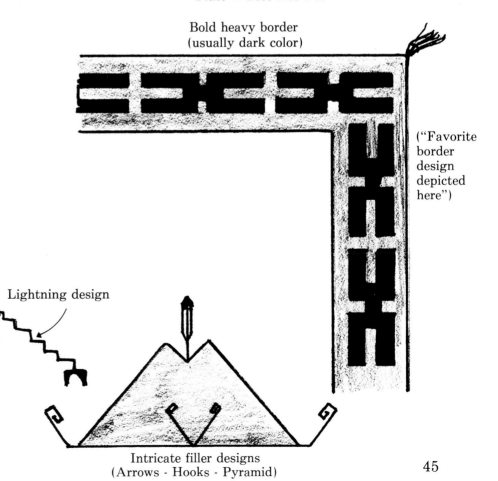

("Favorite
border
design
depicted
here")

Intricate filler designs
(Arrows - Hooks - Pyramid)

45

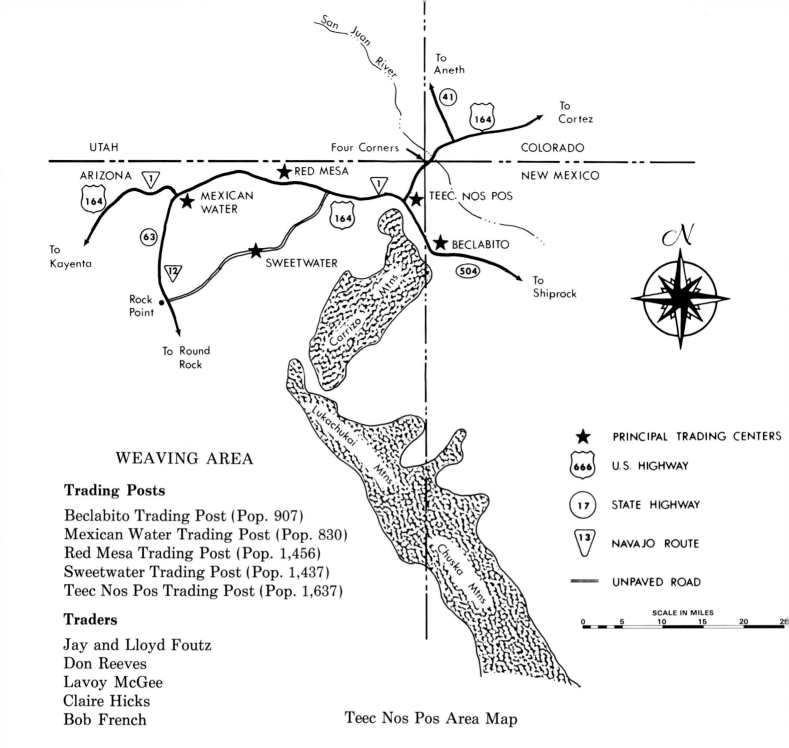

Teec Nos Pos Area Map

WEAVING AREA

Trading Posts

Beclabito Trading Post (Pop. 907)
Mexican Water Trading Post (Pop. 830)
Red Mesa Trading Post (Pop. 1,456)
Sweetwater Trading Post (Pop. 1,437)
Teec Nos Pos Trading Post (Pop. 1,637)

Traders

Jay and Lloyd Foutz
Don Reeves
Lavoy McGee
Claire Hicks
Bob French

WEAVERS

Dorothy Begay	Mary Long (combination Teec Nos Pos and Yei weaver)	Connie Yabenay
Hilda Begay		Emma Yabenay
Nellie T. Begay		Ruth Yabenay
Louise Cattleman	Alice Nelson	Lola Yazzie (combination Teec Nos Pos and Yei weaver)
Lilly Joan	Marie Wallace	
Mary C. Joe	Mary White	

COMPARATIVE COSTS
(Range: $20-$100 per Square Foot)

Year	3 x 5	4 x 6	6 x 9	Large Specials
1964	$100-250	$150-400	$500-1000	$1500 & Up
1974	$150-450	$300-650	$650-2000	$2500 & Up

Crystal — "Where Crystal Water Flows Out".

Chapter 6

Crystal

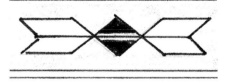

Elevation: 7550'
Post Office Established: 1903
Owner-Trader: Don Jensen

THE POST

On September 3, 1849, Lieutenant James H. Simpson, diarist for the famed Navajo Reconnaissance Expedition under Colonel John M. Washington, included in his entry for that day, ... *I noticed towering pines and firs, also the oak, the aspen, and the willow; and bordering the stream was a great variety of shrubbery, the hop vine, loaded with its fruit, being intertwined among them. Flowers of rich profusion, and of every hue and*

47

delicacy, were also constantly before the eye — upwards of ninety varieties having been picked up since we entered the gorge yesterday. Indeed we are all in hopes that, yesterday and today, we have been having an earnest [view] of what we may yet behold in this part of the world — a rich, well-timbered, and sufficiently-watered country . . . [18] Such was the description of the area the Indians called *Tonlt'ili,* meaning "where crystal water flows out." Here at the west entrance to Washington Pass, the only east-west corridor through the Chuska Mountains, lies the post of Crystal. [19] Blessed with a rare combination of beautiful red-rock buttes interspaced with mountain greenery, the location was long a favored campsite — but not in winter. *"The mountain plain was very pleas-*

Archibald Sweetland (fourth from left) at his Sehili post, circa 1890. (Ben Wittick photo, courtesy: Photograph Collections, Museum of New Mexico).

48

ant in summer," wrote Thomas Keam to Interior Secretary Henry M. Teller in 1884, *"but entirely impracticable in winter, as it is one of the coldest places on the reservation. [I] was told that eighteen inches of snow fell there on the last of April. Whoever recommended [the sheep ranch] never visited the place in winter, when it is often covered with two feet of snow.* [20]

The success of early Navajo trading ventures did not generally include mountain bases. The seasonal handicaps were just too much. Some operations did well when herders brought their flocks to graze the high country meadows but deep snows which lay from October to late spring meant disaster. Several made a run at it though, including Archibald Sweetland who sat out many a lonely hour in a log post called Sehili located high on the west slopes of the Chuskas, twenty-five miles north of Washington Pass. The Sehili site housed a series of owners before its final abandonment on November 14, 1892. Like Sehili, Washington Pass was also a formidable location, but the east-west traffic in good weather warranted a greater risk. A Spanish-American from Fort Defiance, Romulo Martinez, was the first known trader in the pass, in 1873; Ben Hyatt gave it a try between 1882 and 1884; Stephen Aldrich and his partner, Elias Clark, lasted one season (1884), Clark and Charles Hubbell were trading in Washington Pass in 1885. Charles was a younger brother of Juan Lorenzo. Walter Fales came in 1885, and Michael Donovan took over in 1886. There never was an air of permanence about the early Washington Pass merchants. Their trading was probably from tents, and then only during the summer months. John B. Moore, from Sheridan, Wyoming, was different. A slender, balding Irishman, resembling more the likes of an eastern schoolmaster than an Indian trader, he found the Chuska climate to his liking. He purchased the present trading site from Joe Reitz, who with a partner named Wilkin, had traded at the location since 1894. Moore went to work; he cut and hauled timber from the mountains and built himself a log post; he freighted in supplies from the railhead at Gallup, New Mexico, and stocked his shelves with goods. The date of his license showed June 29, 1896.

John B. Moore's mail order catalog, *The Navajo,* 1911. (Courtesy: Gallup, New Mexico, Public Library).

He called the place Crystal and he was open for business — and what a business it was! Moore endured the long months of winter isolation by employing Navajo weavers to make rugs for him. He originated designs, improved the wool for spinning, and encouraged quality weaving. Almost immediately, he established himself as a master trader with a reputation for dealing in fine rugs. He developed a characteristic regional style pattern and publicized the craftsmanship of his weavers by publishing a mail order catalog. By the early 1900's the business was flourishing, with his rugs becoming known all over the country.

Moore's basic philosophy and ultimate success is perhaps revealed in the foreword to his catalog, *The Navajo.*

THE NAVAJO Indian rug or blanket, no longer a mere curio, is now an article of real

By permission Sim. Schwemberger.
CRYSTAL, NAVAJO RESERVATION, NEW MEXICO.
In front of the store.

By permission Sim. Schwemberger.
CRYSTAL, NAVAJO RESERVATION, NEW MEXICO.
Inside view of store.

Scenes at Crystal Trading Post, circa 1911.

Bottom: Inside the store; John B. Moore (facing camera) on left, beside Manager, Jesse A. Molohon. **Top:** In front of the post. Manager Molohon holding Indian child; Moore, second from right.

(Reprinted from *The Navajo*, 1911, courtesy: Gallup, New Mexico, Public Library).

service so well known and extensively used that it is not intended here to go into any general and lengthy description of it. It is one of the writer's concerns, that he has played a part in its introduction equal to that of any other; and firm conviction, that his part in bringing it up to its present high standard of excellence, so fully deserving the high esteem in which it is now held; is second to that of no other. Beginning some fifteen years back as an Indian trader in a rather small way, I have labored unceasingly with and among these Navajo weavers, inducing them to weave better, finer, cleaner and handsomer rugs on the one hand; and just as persistently on the other, to convince the buying public of the real worth and better value of this better product.

In the light of past experience, I doubt if I would enter again on the proposition if set back to the time of beginning. But once in it, have never been able yet to find a place where I could quit. It has not been easy. In the beginning I had stubborn and conservative workers in these Navajo women, and a discredited product to contend with on one hand; and on the other, a prejudice and lack of knowledge that has proved harder to break down and overcome than I had anticipated.

But, measured by results, I have not failed in either. My weavers are today making more and finer rugs than ever in their history, and their work is selling more readily, and at prices partially proportioned to its better value, than ever before. Resistance, stubborn, hurtful, and senseless opposition on the part of the weavers, has given place to cheerful co-operation, good natured rivalry and friendly strife for excellence in their work. Prejudice and indifference on the part of the public, is giving way to active interest and a substantial demand when and wherever my fine rugs are let in to plead their own cause.

Not the least part of my satisfaction in what has been accomplished, is the greatly increased prosperity and better conditions of life that has come to the people among whom I live and work, as their earning power has grown. But, I am no philanthropist and must disclaim any philanthropic motives for my part in it. I saw, or at least believed that I saw, in their dormant skill and patience a business opportunity, provided they could be aroused, encouraged and led on to do their best; and a market for their product could be

established. It seemed my one best business proposition at the time and I played it, realizing, that if I would prosper myself I must help my workers to prosper too — if they prospered, that I would come in for a share with them at least.

And now, I am seeking your business on precisely this same basis and no other. If you ever should buy a Navajo rug, I propose making it to your interest to buy of me. For every dollar of your money that I ask, expect or may ever get; I pledge you full value and more than it will buy in like quality and quantity from any other. More: I promise you a quality that no price whatever will secure from another, unless it comes first from me, and at a RIGHT PRICE TOO.

This claim is not intended as a knock on anybody's goods. Any good Navajo rug is worth all you pay for it no matter from whom you buy it. But MY fine ones are a REAL and not a claimed specialty. They are in a class by themselves — no other has their like and there is no competition in them. There is just the one BEST quality, and that is the J. B. MOORE rugs, woven exclusively for him by the Crystal, N. Mex. colony of Navajo weavers. Our weavers are better paid than any others, but they do better work and that is WHY they do it. Our finest rugs may be higher priced than those of some others, but they are finer and better worth their price. And, you cannot get their equal from any other at any price unless, it may be from some one who first bought them here.

You are not asked or expected to accept my bare statement for this. See the goods and then decide. I will ship on approval and if you are not wholly satisfied, ship back at my expense. This is the kind my rugs are. I gladly take all risk of return expense for the chance of having you see them. A satisfied customer is worth more to me than any one sale. He or she, frequently come back with re-orders. At least, they will not turn away from me friends who may want similar goods. [22]

Moore sold his holdings in late 1911 to his manager of three years, Jesse A. Molohon.[23] From 1919 to 1922 the post was in the chain of Gallup trading magnate C. C. Manning. Manning's clerk, Charlie Newcomb, was an owner until 1936, followed by J. B. Collyer. Don Jensen, the present owner, began trading at the famous old post in 1944.

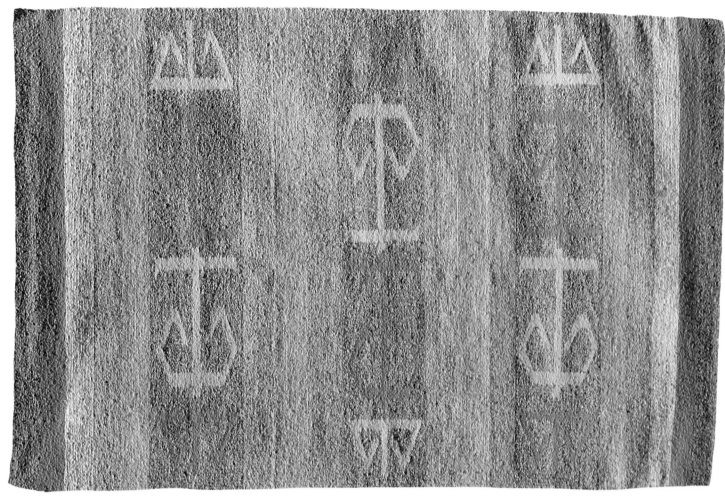

Plate 9. Crystal

THE RUG

The early Crystal rug of Moore's design was a bordered product designed with crosses, diamonds, terraces, a characteristic hook and fork pattern, along with swastikas and arrows. The Moore line was generously embellished with aniline red and to lesser degrees, with outlines of blue.

When Moore left the Reservation in 1911, the quality rugs that he originated ended shortly thereafter. His basic designs, however, continued to flourish for a number of years in the Two Gray Hills district to the east. From the grave of the pre-Revival Crystal, however, rose a new rug type. Dating from the early 1940's, the "new" Crystal departed radically from its predecessor, and, as it marched into the Regional Style Period, (under the guidance of Jensen), it became extremely popular.

There is no mistaking the modern Crystal. It is one of the most distinctive and beautifully woven of all the styles on the Reservation. The rug is borderless and is composed of rich, all-vegetal, earth-toned hues of brown, gold, and orange, with subtle touches of green, gray and maroon. The basic pattern is Early Classic Period stripes and bands that are horizontally paneled with a characteristic "wavy line" technique, an effect created by alternating two or three wefts of contrasting color. The appeal of the Crystal rivals that of the Two Gray Hills from across the mountains mainly because its pleasing tones are so functional in contemporary home decorating.

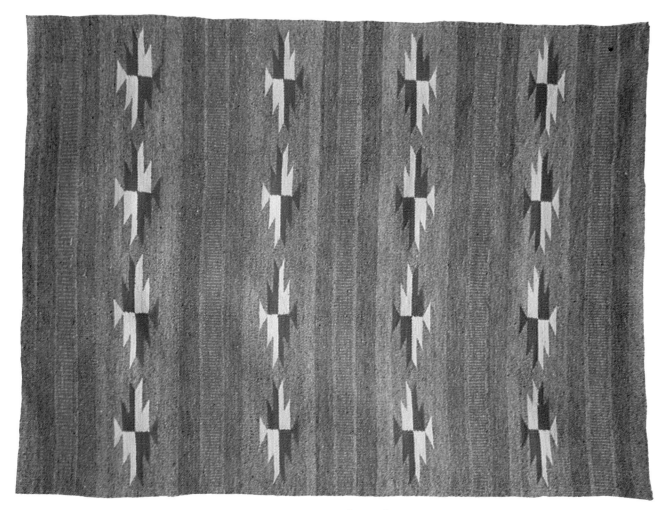

Plate 10. Crystal

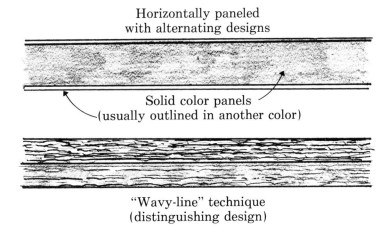

Horizontally paneled
with alternating designs

Solid color panels
(usually outlined in another color)

"Wavy-line" technique
(distinguishing design)

Crystal Designs

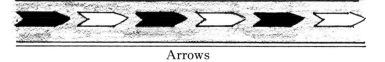

Arrows

Feathers
(Sometimes corn stalks are used)

Stacked diamonds

53

Borderless

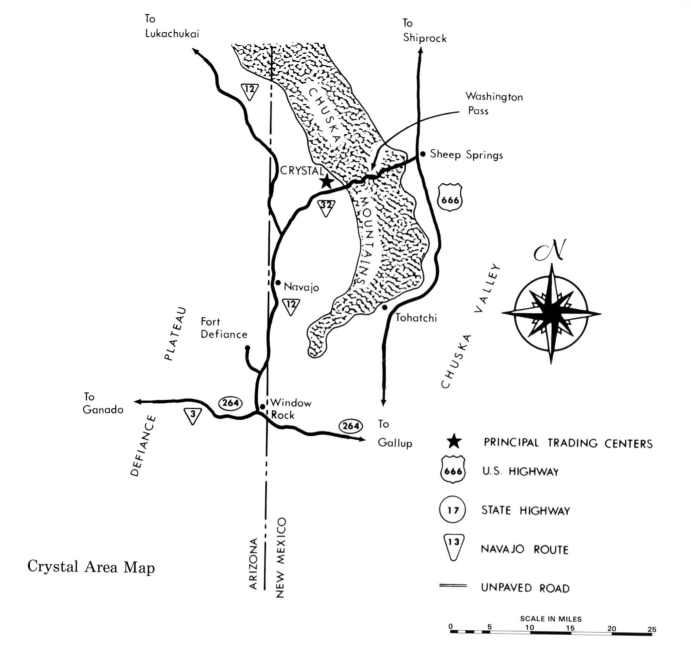

Crystal Area Map

PRINCIPAL TRADING CENTERS ★

U.S. HIGHWAY (666)

STATE HIGHWAY (17)

NAVAJO ROUTE (13)

UNPAVED ROAD ═══

SCALE IN MILES
0   5   10   15   20   25

WEAVING AREA

Trading Post

Crystal Trading Post (Pop. 833)

Trader

Don Jensen

WEAVERS

Margaret Begay   Jennett Tsosie
Rachael Begay   Mary Wingate
Mary Moore

COMPARATIVE COSTS
(Range: $20-$100 per Square Foot)

Year	3 x 5	4 x 6	6 x 9	Large Specials
1964	$50-150	$200-350	$400-650	$1000 & Up
1974	$100-300	$300-750	$500-1000	$1500 & Up

Two Gray Hills — From the Chaco wastelands comes the Reservation's costliest rug.

Chapter 7

Two Gray Hills

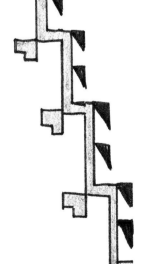

Elevation: 5920'
Trader: Derald Stock
Owners: Mrs. Willard Leighton and Derald Stock

THE POST

The road is rocky coming in from the east and you don't actually see the post until a small rise is topped about half a mile distant. The first impression is usually disappointment. "Is that it?" many have remarked. "Are you sure?" Such is one's introduction to the home and place name of the Reservation's most prized rug, the Two Gray Hills.

Situated on a treeless pediment separating the Chuska Mountains to the west from the Chaco wastelands, the site appears on 19th century maps as Crozier.[24] The name, Two Gray Hills, was probably derived from the Indian name, *Bis dahlitso*, which means, "upper yellow adobe."[25] Actually, there are several hills which backdrop the post and the color is tan, not gray.

55

Plate 11. Two Gray Hills

Plate 12. Two Gray Hills

In the spring of 1897, a year after he sold the Crystal post to John B. Moore, Joe Wilkin joined forces with Frank and Henry Noel and started a new post on the east side of the Chuskas. Business was a struggle at first, and the solitude of the site was at times almost unbearable. Henry Noel spoke often of the early years at Two Gray Hills, recalling one winter in which he and his horse appeared to be the only living things in the valley. Observing the coralled animal for perhaps an hour through blizzard skies, he remarked that the horse was probably as lonely and wretched as he was.

Brother Frank sold out his interests in 1900 to Henry and another brother, H. B. Noel, who had recently come west for his health. In 1902, the trading venture passed into the hands of Win Wetherill. H. B. Noel stayed on for awhile before striking out on his own into the Teec Nos Pos area. Two years later, the post changed hands again when it was bought by Wilkin's former partner, Joe Reitz.

Two years before John B. Moore departed from Crystal, an Englishman named Ed Davies bought into the Two Gray Hills post with Reitz. A year later, George Bloomfield set up shop five miles west at a site called Toadlena, a corruption of the Indian name, *Tohaali,* meaning "water bubbling up." With the collapse of Moore's rug dynasty at Crystal, some of his original designs filtered eastward through the snowy confines of Washington Pass to be nourished by the Two Gray Hills weavers. The area women eliminated Moore's bright colors, especially the red, and began to produce a distinctive rug of their own. By 1925, the design elements borrowed from Moore had disappeared. Davies, now sole owner at Two Gray Hills, and Bloomfield were responsible for this, as they spent many patient hours pointing out to their weavers the fine points of individual style and quality craftsmanship. What resulted from the efforts of these two dedicated traders was emergence of one of the finest textile styles to come — and which continues to come — from the post-Revival loom, the Two Gray Hills rug.

Vic Walker followed Davies at Two Gray Hills in 1938; Walter Scribner had a partner interest in 1941. Mr. and Mrs. Willard Leighton purchased the post in 1948 and continued the efforts of their predecessors to maintain the quality and reputation of the rug. In 1972, the manager of the store, Derald Stock, acquired an interest in the post.

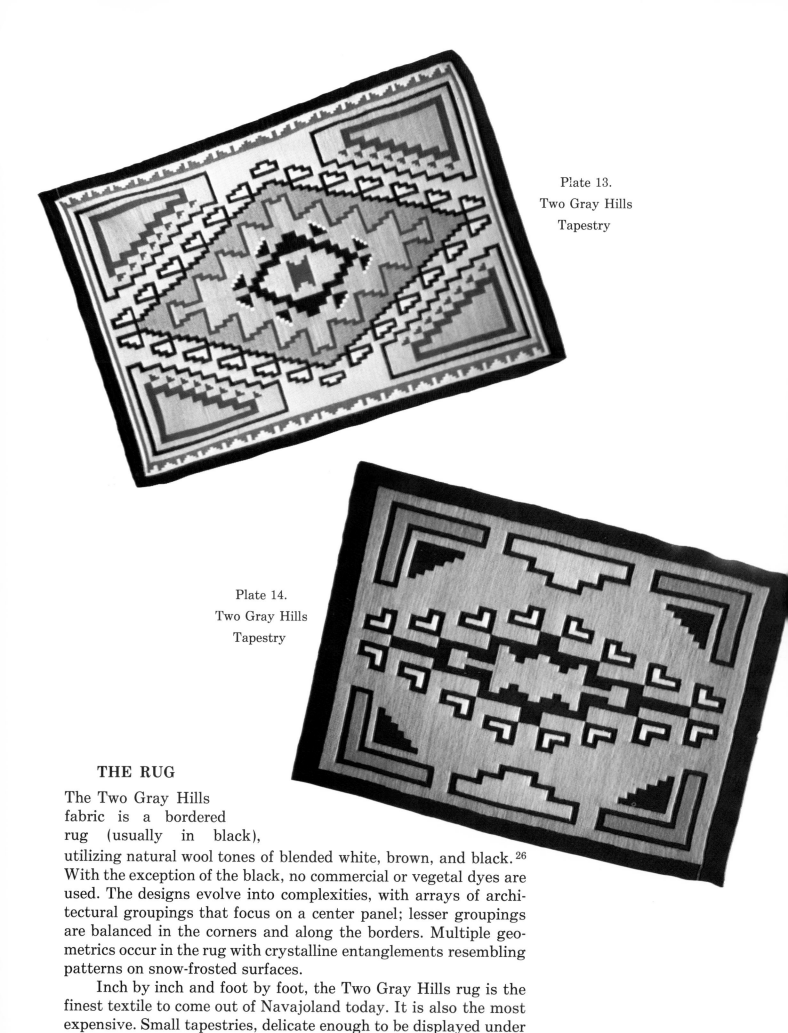

Plate 13.
Two Gray Hills
Tapestry

Plate 14.
Two Gray Hills
Tapestry

THE RUG

The Two Gray Hills
fabric is a bordered
rug (usually in black),
utilizing natural wool tones of blended white, brown, and black.[26]
With the exception of the black, no commercial or vegetal dyes are
used. The designs evolve into complexities, with arrays of archi-
tectural groupings that focus on a center panel; lesser groupings
are balanced in the corners and along the borders. Multiple geometrics occur in the rug with crystalline entanglements resembling
patterns on snow-frosted surfaces.

Inch by inch and foot by foot, the Two Gray Hills rug is the
finest textile to come out of Navajoland today. It is also the most
expensive. Small tapestries, delicate enough to be displayed under
glass, have sold for as much as $7,000. One of the most attractive

58

Plate 15. Two Gray Hills Tapestry

Plate 16. Two Gray Hills Tapestry

characteristics of the finer rugs is the light weight, accounted for by ex-extremely careful carding and spinning, resulting in a high thread count in weaving. A weft count of 100 or more generally qualifies a rug as a tapestry. Some of the outstanding examples of Two Gray Hills rugs count in excess of 120 wefts to the inch. This is amazing when 30-50 wefts to the inch is considered a good Navajo rug.

A short distance north of Two Gray Hills lies a small trading center called Tocito (Navajo, meaning "hot springs."). Here a small group of weavers are recalling some of Moore's early examples and have begun modifying the standard Two Gray Hills natural wool tones by inserting some aniline dyes into the weave. Turquoise, or combinations of green and blue, appear to be favorite colors with the Tocito group; some examples reveal rust shades. In a subtle manner, the dyed yarn will occupy the center eye of the pattern with possibly lesser usages in the corner panels.

At Sanostee, (Navajo, meaning "rocks around it") Trading Post, located off U.S. 666 to the north toward Shiprock, another refinement is taking place in the Two Gray Hills weave. The Sanostee women are incorporating vegetal dyes to match the blended wool tones of the standard Two Gray Hills colors (beige, brown, tan and gray). This relatively new approach is resulting in some very attractive pieces. Some debate has been prompted by the Sanostee techniques, since some rug "purists" refuse to accept the textile as a true Two Gray Hills.

It is interesting to note that the one active male weaver on the Navajo Reservation, James Sherman, is located at Two Gray Hills. A quality weaver, Mr. Sherman's work is always in demand by collectors.

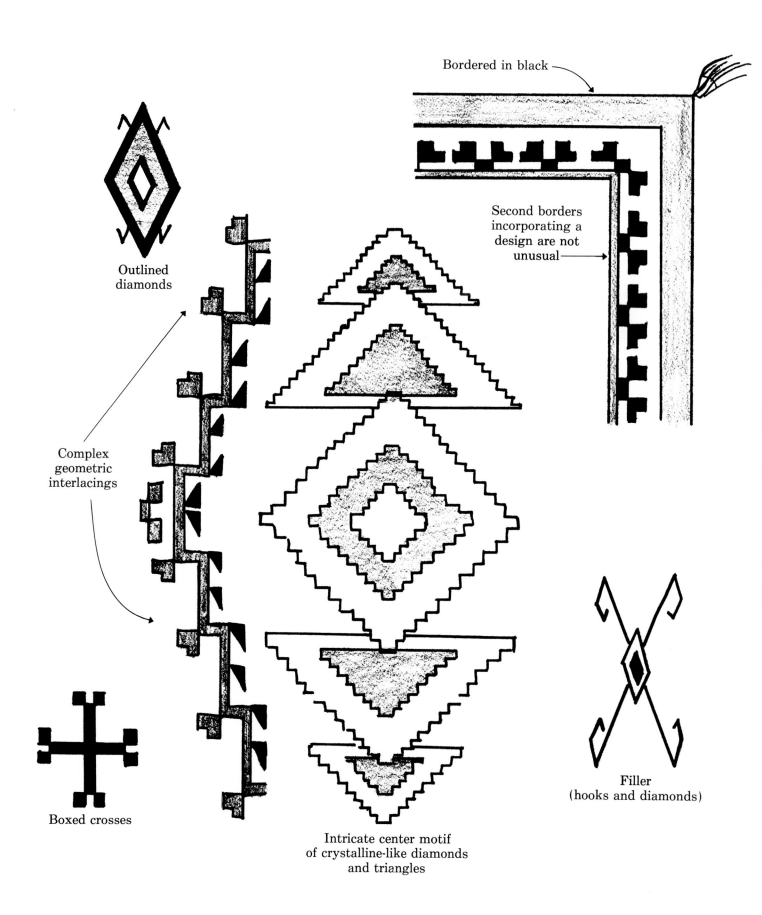

Outlined
diamonds

Complex
geometric
interlacings

Bordered in black

Second borders
incorporating a
design are not
unusual

Filler
(hooks and diamonds)

Boxed crosses

Intricate center motif
of crystalline-like diamonds
and triangles

Two Gray Hills Designs

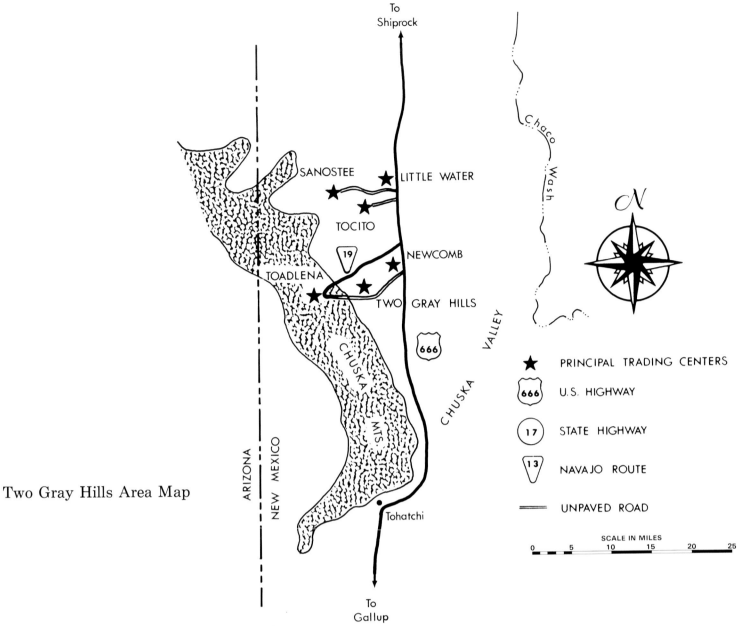

Two Gray Hills Area Map

WEAVING AREA

Trading Posts	Traders
Little Water Trading Post	R. B. Foutz, Jr.
Newcomb Trading Post	R. B. Foutz, Jr.
Sanostee Trading Post	Monroe Foutz
Toadlena Trading Post	R. B. Foutz, Jr.
Tocito Trading Post (closed)	R. B. Foutz, Jr.
Two Gray Hills Trading Post (Pop. 2,448)	Derald Stock

WEAVERS

Cora Curley	Rose Mike	Mary Teal
Julia Jumbo	Elisabeth Mute	Ruth Teller
Marie Laphie	Mildred Natoni	Mary Tom
Marie Little Joe	Clara Sherman	Daisy Togelechee
Dorothy Mike	James Sherman	Margaret Yazzie

COMPARATIVE COSTS

(Range: $20-$300 per Square Foot)

Year	3 x 5	4 x 6	6 x 9	Large Specials
1964	$ 100-350	$ 200-500	$ 750-1200	$3000 & Up
1974	$250-1000	$500-1500	$2000-5000	$6000 & Up

61

Thunderbird Lodge at Chinle — oasis at the mouth of the canyon.

Chapter 8

Chinle
"It flows from the canyon"

Elevation: 5058'
Post Office Established: 1903
Owners-Traders: Mrs. Camilo (Pauline) Garcia and Gerald LaFont
(Thunderbird Lodge)

THE POST

Since the beginning of the 17th century, the magnificent canyon called de Chelly (Spanish corruption of the Navajo word "tseghi," meaning "rock canyon," with the English pronunciation a further corruption from the Spanish), has held a special place in the hearts of all Navajos. A tributary canyon called Canyon del Mureto ("canyon of the dead") was witness to the Spanish massacre of Navajo women, children and old men in 1805. Some 40 years later, Colonel Washington is alleged to have burned hogans in his approach to the canyon, although the Navajos themselves may have set fire to them as they fled. Following this, in 1864, came Kit Carson's troops during the bitterly remembered "Navajo Roundup."

The deep, thousand-foot chasms of the canyon offer protection; the bottomlands serve as excellent farms; the juniper and piñon forested rims yield timber and fuel; and the soil affords limited grazing. The canyons were sparsely occupied from about A.D. 1300 until arrival of Navajos in the region. The exact date of their occupation has not yet been established. It was a natural site for trade purposes.

The first known merchant was a Mexican, a non-licensed trader named Naakaii Yazzie, who operated out of a tent in 1882. The first valid license was issued to Juan Lorenzo Hubbell, of Ganado, and his partner, C. N. Cotton, early in 1886. Business was poor at the first Chinle store, and Hubbell let his operating license lapse the following year.[28]

Several traders followed Juan Lorenzo into the three-room rock hogan that he built:

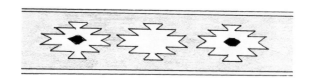

Sam Day's Chinle Trading Post, circa 1890. Thunderbird Lodge now occupies the site.
(Ben Wittick photo, courtesy: Photograph Collection, Museum of New Mexico).

Mike Donovan in 1887, Thomas J. Lingle (1888), Bernard J. Mooney and James F. Boyle (1889), and John W. Boehm in 1889.

In 1900, Hubbell returned to Chinle and constructed a second post on the site of the present post office. Realizing the tourist potential of Canyon de Chelly, Hubbell built an elaborate two-story rock hostel to accommodate guests; the floor level serving as the trading post. Hubbell's foresight for tourism was correct, but it was about 30 years premature. The "no cars — no roads" environment of the Reservation forced a second withdrawal in 1918 when he sold the holdings to his partner, Cotton.

In 1902, a veteran trader named Sam Day moved in and established a log store a short distance south of the mouth of Canyon de Chelly. This store, a forerunner of the now-existing Thunderbird Lodge was sold in 1905 to Charles F. Weidemeyer.

The Chinle trading area was for a time operating with three different posts. It was a bit crowded to say the least, and none of the owners were realizing much from the divided business. The situation was improved in 1923 when a tri-partnership of Camilo Garcia, Leon H. (Cozy) McSparron, and Hartley T. Seymour bought all three posts. They closed down Hubbell's old rock mansion and concentrated their business back at the mouth of the canyon. Camilo Garcia assumed sole ownership in later years, and the existing store stands today on Hubbell's original 1886 site. The same applies to Sam Day's (Thunderbird Lodge) plot of land, located one mile south, where Gerald LaFont now operates.

Garcia's Trading Post at Chinle, circa 1949. (Jack Snow photo, M. Burge Collection, courtesy: Photograph Collection, Museum of New Mexico).

Plate 17.

Chinle

THE RUG

Trader Leon H. (Cozy) McSparron is responsible for the Chinle style rug. His experiments with dyes, both vegetal and commercial, provided impetus to his weavers to revive the simple stripes and bands of the Early Classic Period (1700-1850). The modern Chinle rug has maintained the McSparron suggestion and today reflects the combination of both vegetal and aniline dyes. It is generally considered, however, that the contemporary Chinle is basically vegetal. Commercial dyes are used sparingly to outline or accentuate the smaller designs. The borderless rug has a spacious feeling with small terraced designs and squash blossoms encased in broad bands. Some of the intervening stripes use the

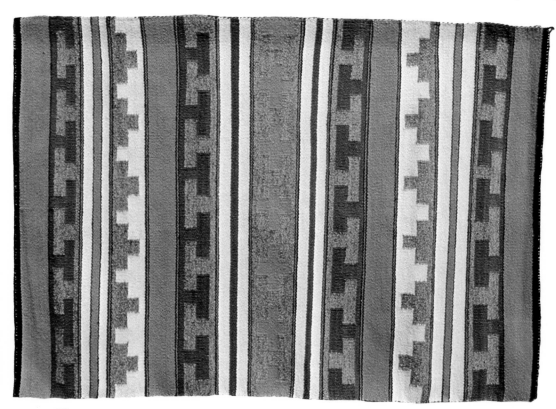

Plate 18.

Chinle

Crystal "wavy line" technique. The weavers in the district create an attractive rug of pleasing balance. Natural white wool usually provides the background, with less used shades of vegetal-dyed green, brown, and gray. Rose colors and yellows are favorites, along with aniline black to denote outlines and termination panels at the ends. The rug is distinctive and well-woven. Some pieces must be closely examined to distinguish them from a Crystal or a Wide Ruins. One of the keys is the color utilization, part vegetal and part aniline. Also, the weave is somewhat heavier than its all-vegetal neighbors.

A small trading post called Nazlini, located 20 miles south of Chinle, has prompted a few arguments among rug experts in recent years. Some writers feel that the Nazlini craftswomen weave a style that is distinctive enough to warrant regional recognition. The rug, known as a "Nazlini," is in essence an unbordered Ganado, exhibiting a combination of vegetal dyes and commercial colorants, particularly red. Prior to the 1950's, weavers of the district produced rugs exclusively in the Ganado style (red-black-gray-white). Some references credit a missionary-trader named Goss with influencing the weavers to take up vegetal dyeing.[29] The end result is that the so-called "Nazlini," being located halfway between Chinle and Ganado, actually reflects the style and colors of both areas in a pleasing combination. The basic design, however, is more aligned with Chinle characteristics, therefore is acknowledged in this chapter.

Horizontally paneled
with alternating designs

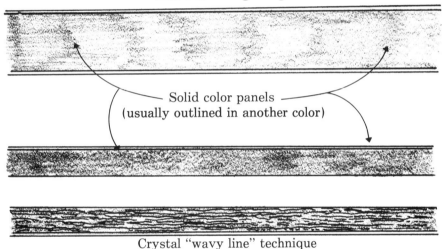

Solid color panels
(usually outlined in another color)

Crystal "wavy line" technique

Chinle Designs

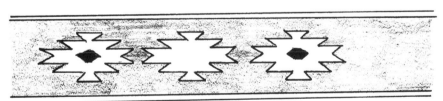

Squash blossom designs
(favorite Chinle design)

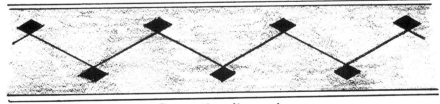

Connecting diamonds

Borderless

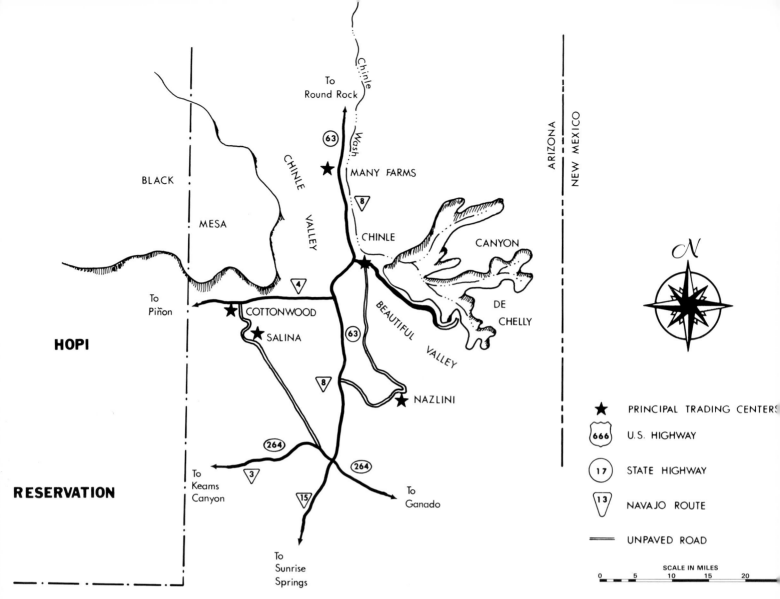

Chinle Area Map

WEAVING AREA

Trading Posts

Cottonwood Trading Post
Garcia Trading Post (Chinle, Pop. 4,195)
Many Farms Trading Post (Pop. 1,529)
Nazlini Trading Post (Pop. 1,713)
Salina Trading Post (Pop. 1,797)
Thunderbird Lodge (Chinle)

Traders

Ernest Gormon
Charles Weleck
Glen Osterfelt
Alan Carson
Dave Murray
Gerald LaFont

WEAVERS

Jessie Gorman	Suzie Hunter	Elisabeth Stewart
Ason Tsosie Hayou	Lorene Nez	Sarah Van Winkle
Rita Hayou	Lana Spencer	Rose Yazzie

COMPARATIVE COSTS
(Range: $10-$25 per Square Foot)

Year	3 x 5	4 x 6	6 x 9	Large Specials
1964	$40-100	$100-200	$250-350	$500 & Up
1974	$75-150	$250-350	$400-750	$1000 & Up

Hubbell's — the home of a trading empire.

Chapter 9

Ganado

Elevation: 6400'
Post Office Established: 1883
Trader: W. S. (Bill) Young
Owner: U.S. National Park Service

THE POST

"There was an aura of history and permanence about Ganado [Hubbells] that no other trading post could achieve. It was not only the long dim store with high counters, whose only light came through two barred windows at the front, it was memories of other times" — Elizabeth Compton Hegemann *(University of New Mexico Press, 1963).*

Ganado (Spanish meaning "herd of cattle") is situated on the crimson shale plains midway between the Defiance Plateau on the east and the Hopi mesas to the west. The main trading center is nestled in a small valley along the southern banks of Pueblo Colorado Wash, 28 miles west of Window Rock on Arizona Highway 264 (Navajo Route 3).

The first settlement in the area dates back at least to Basketmaker III times, around the 8th century, and possibly even earlier. Ancestors to some of the Hopi Indians probably occupied the Wide Reeds site, a

Juan Lorenzo Hubbell, circa 1890. (Courtesy: Photograph Collection, Museum of New Mexico).

communal dwelling nearby, in the 13th century. The first trading post, called Pueblo Colorado (Spanish meaning "red village"), was established by Charles Crary in 1871. W. B. "Old Man" Leonard traded at the location between the years 1876-1878 before selling out to Juan Lorenzo Hubbell. Hubbell, in honor of his friend and Navajo chieftan Ganado Mucho (Spanish meaning "many cattle") is responsible for the current place name. From this headquarters, Juan Lorenzo later formed a partnership with C. N. Cotton, then sold out entirely to the latter. By 1899 Hubbell was again the owner, and he built a trading empire which eventually encompassed 14 trading posts, wholesale warehousing, and freighting. His reputation gained the title, "the greatest of all Indian traders." Juan Lorenzo Hubbell managed his vast holdings for over three decades. When he died on November 11, 1930, responsibility for the property was assumed by his son, Roman, who carried on until his death in October, 1957. His wife, Dorothy, continued the family managership until 1967. Hubbell Hill, a conical shaped promontory north of the post, serves as the family ceme-

Interior of Hubbell Trading Post warehouse, circa 1890.
(Courtesy: Swenson-Lesh Collection, Photograph Collection, Museum of New Mexico).

tery plot, bearing the remains of Lorenzo, Sr., his wife, Lina Rubi; two sons, Lorenzo, Jr., and Roman; a daughter, Adele; and Many Horses, a Navajo family friend.

On April 3, 1967, Hubbell Trading Post was purchased by the U.S. Government to be operated as a National Historic Site. It is one of the few National Park Service installations that functions largely in the manner which warranted its preservation — trading with the Indians. Today, Park Service guides conduct regular tours through the old Hubbell home, the post, and surrounding grounds.

Under Park Service management the Southwest Parks and Monuments Association operates the post as a living history exhibit, a trading post carrying on the old tradition so well exemplified by Juan Lorenzo Hubbell.

THE RUG

The famed Ganado "red" is perhaps the best known of all Navajo rugs, considered by most non-Indians what a Navajo rug should look like. Its creator, Juan Lorenzo Hubbell, specialized in a well-woven product that featured a brilliant red background surrounded

The post.

The bull pen.

The home.

by strong geometric crosses, diamonds, and stripes colored with yarns of gray, white, and black. Hubbell's influence is still very much in evidence in the modern Ganado. The central motif is usually a bold diamond or cross, sometimes outlined in another color. Smaller forms occupy the remaining spaces. The rug can range from large, simple, bold designs to intricate, more sophisticated works. The bright reds are still the dominant characteristic throughout the pattern, although recently the tones have taken on rich shades of burgundy. In some contemporary examples, various shades of gray are replacing the red backgrounds. The average Ganado, while usually of area rug size, has a modern-day tendency to feature smaller tapestry types for wall hangings.

Although bordered on the south by the vegetal-dye centers, the Ganado is a combina-

tion of the natural colors (grays and whites), the aniline dyes of black, and the characteristic red.

Two areas identifed with the Ganado but sometimes subdivided into separate regional style centers, are Klagetoh to the south, and Piñon to the west. The familiar red-black-gray-white influence is evident in both. In contemporary weaves, neither Klagetoh nor Piñon has achieved the individualism to warrant regional recognition. Weavers in the Piñon-Keams Canyon area during the late Revival Period became famous for their huge loom products, one measuring as much as 24 x 36 feet. Some rug experts feel that this size trait is sufficient to separate Piñon from the rest of the styles. However, in studying the early Ganados, large sizes were one of the chief characteristics.

From the Klagetoh "namers" comes further confusion. Located 12 miles south of Ganado, Klagetoh Trading Post has achieved some measure of publicity from retailers calling a certain type of Ganado a "Klagetoh". Here, as in the Piñon area, the same red-black-gray-white rug prevails. Some current arguments insist that the "klagetoh" is more sophisticated than the Ganado; that there is more design and complication in pattern; utilization of both vegetal and aniline dyes; elimination of the Classic crosses and diamonds; less red, more black, and so forth. Carelessness in rug naming continues farther when even the "Klagetoh" is subdivided. Twenty miles to the northwest, a small iso-

The rug room.

lated post called Sunrise Springs has recently found itself named in recognition of a certain serrated diamond-type rug. In all cases, the final answer was the fertile mind of Juan Lorenzo Hubbell. His influence on Navajo weaving styles touched a greater geographic sphere than was originally considered. Today, that sphere of influence is still growing. Far to the north, at the gateway to Monument Valley, some Kayenta weavers are producing excellent red-black-gray-white rugs in typical Ganado designs. Some writers or enterprising retailers, are apparently attempting to devise a new regional style rug to be called a "Kayenta". The only different traits in the rug are white backgrounds (instead of red) and smaller designs.

Plate 19. Unfinished Ganado on the loom.

Plate 21. Ganado

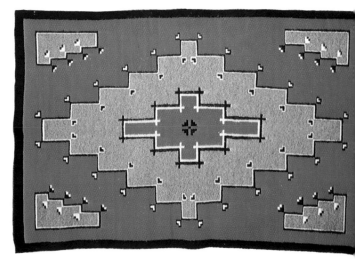

Plate 22. Ganado

Plate 20. Ganado

Plate 23. Ganado

Open cross

Encased cross

Outlined diamonds

Bordered
(usually in black)

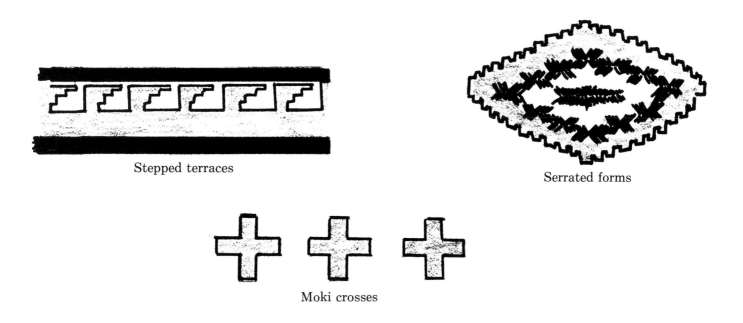

Stepped terraces

Serrated forms

Moki crosses

Ganado Designs

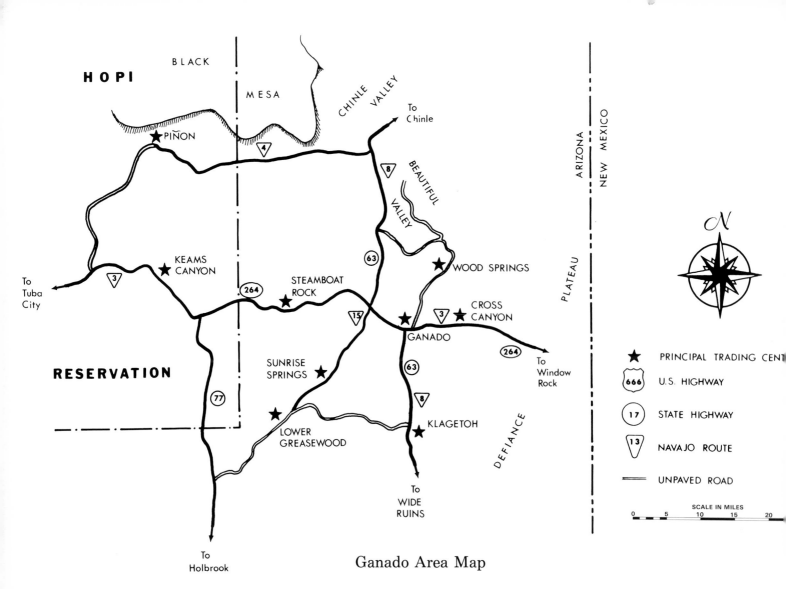

Ganado Area Map

WEAVING AREA

Trading Posts	Traders
Cross Canyon Trading Post	John Barr
Hubbell Trading Post (Ganado, Pop. 984)	W. S. (Bill) Young
Keams Canyon Trading Post	William H. McGee
Klagetoh Trading Post (Pop. 1,419)	Jerrold B. Foutz
Lower Greasewood Trading Post (Pop. 1,329)	Clarence A. Wheeler
Piñon Trading Post (Pop. 3,352)	William H. McGee
Steamboat Rock Trading Post (Pop. 1,258)	Jerrold B. Foutz
Sunrise Springs Trading Post	Clarence A. Wheeler
Wood Springs Trading Post	Guy Morgan

WEAVERS

Louise Begay	Mary Curley	Mary Reed
Marilyn Begay	Lucy James	Mary T. Wilson
Sadie Begay	Mary Jones	Sadie Yazzie

COMPARATIVE COSTS
(Range: $20-$100 per Square Foot)

Year	3 x 5	4 x 6	6 x 9	Large Specials
1964	$50-100	$100-300	$300-500	$500 & Up
1974	$75-500	$500-900	$900-1500	$1500 & Up

Wide Ruins — in the hill country of the Anasazi.

Chapter 10

Wide Ruins

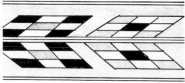

Elevation: 6000'
Post Office
Established: 1934
Owners-Traders: Mr. and Mrs. John Rieffer

THE POST

In the Juniper-forested hill country separating Chinle Valley from the Rio Puerco lies the trading center called Wide Ruins, named for the great Anasazi ruin, Kinteel.

Stillness best describes the location. The buildings are situated off of the main paved road and nestled in a sandy hillock that is hidden from the casual view by the low arms of spreading cottonwood trees. Normally dry

Wide Ruins Wash has carved a colorful rocky swath downhill from the sheep corral and serves as a dividing line separating the post complex from the more modern community and school on a hilltop to the west.

The Wide Ruins post, situated on the grounds of Kinteel, is relatively new in the role of a rug center. Improved north-south roads connecting old U.S. 66 with paralleling Reservation routes are mainly responsible for a series of 20th century trade centers that sprang up in between. At Kinteel, however, trading dates back to post-Bosque Redondo days (1868), where a list of now-forgotten entrepreneurs conducted their barters.[30]

The recordable succession of traders commences in the early 1900's with the names of Spencer Balcomb, Wallace Sanders, and Peter Paquette. Perhaps the most synonymous name associated with Wide Ruins is Lippincott. William Lippincott and his wife, Sallie, recently graduated from the University of Chicago, spent the summer of 1938 as seasonal employees with the National Park Service at Canyon de Chelly. Succumbing to the love of the redrocks, the Lippincotts began to search for an endeavor that would extend their stay. With the assistance and urging of Chinle neighbor, "Cozy" McSparron, they scouted the Indian country for the purchase of a trading post. In October that followed they closed a deal with former Navajo Superintendent, Peter Paquette, for the then called Kinteel Trading Post.

Bill and Sallie Lippincott, circa 1945.
(Photo courtesy: Sallie Wagner).

The Lippincotts deserve the credit for improving and publicizing the rug industry in the southeast corner of the Reservation. Their vegetal dye experiments and encouragement of master weaving resulted in a superior

First Wide Ruins stockade-type post as it lay abandoned in 1906. Remnants of Kinteel ruins on skyline.
(Photo by Loy Turberville, courtesy: John Rieffer).

Wide Ruins rock post at present location, circa 1906.
(Photo by Loy Turberville, courtesy: John Rieffer).

Plate 24. Wide Ruins

79

textile in the years that followed. Sallie kept on hand a current plant recipe book which weavers could consult; Bill promoted a two-room addition to the schoolhouse so that weaving classes could be taught to the younger women — promising to buy their class projects; and jointly, they conceived the idea of holding craft festivals which they hosted in their home, complete with refreshments, home movies, gifts for the children, and awards for the best weaving and silversmithing.[31]

Except for an absence during World War II when Bill served as a naval commander in

ests, and today, the present owners, John and Sharon Rieffer, are continuing efforts to promote a high level of weaving excellence.

THE RUG

The Wide Ruins district is the second all-vegetal dye center on the Reservation; it is also one of the most recent in regional style recognition, being developed by Sallie Lippincott in 1939-40. The quality of the rug owes its origin to a desire of the Lippincotts to revitalize a poor rug market among the area

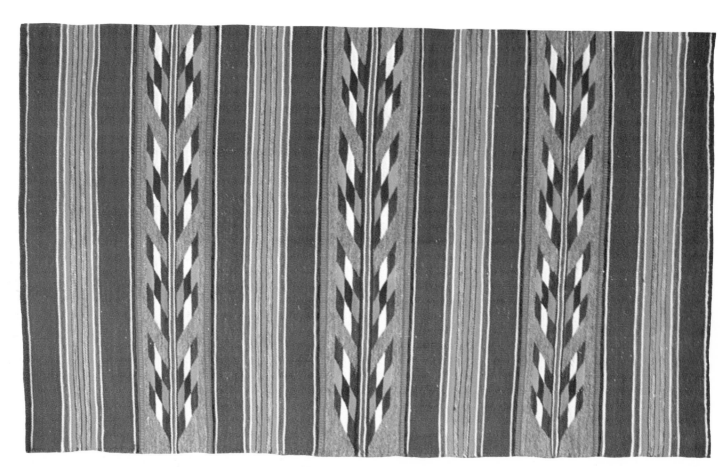

Plate 25. Wide Ruins

San Diego, the popular Lippincotts traded at Wide Ruins until the fall of 1950, when they sold out to the Navajo Tribe.[32] A few years later the Foutz family assumed ownership and the post was operated by Phil Foutz under the banner of Progressive Mercantile. J. B. Collyer, Jr., son of the former Crystal trader, took over in 1957, followed by a partnership in 1964 when John Rieffer bought in. In July, 1973, the former sold out his interests, and today, the present owners, John and

weavers. At Sallie's personal preference and insistence, the traders began their program by announcing that they would no longer buy a rug with a border.[33] Undoubtedly influenced by McSparron and the Chinle success, they discouraged elaborate designs, and instead promoted simple horizontal stripes and bands constructed of total vegetal colors and handspun wool.

The Wide Ruins rugs that are produced

80

today continue in fine workmanship; all hand-spun, beautifully dyed and woven. The natural colors of gray and white are used sparingly, but the blending of subtle shades of seemingly endless plant combinations, defies description. Soft pastels of exquisite pinks, yellows, beige, deep corals, rich grays, olive greens, multiple tones of tans and browns and hues of lilac all combine to make the Wide Ruins rug a popular choice.

To complement the colors, the Wide Ruins weaving design is Early Classic Period stripes and bands situated across a borderless product. Overall simplicity is intended, although ornamentation is quite complex. Finely constructed outlines, hatch work, "wavy line" insertions, and beading techniques usually provide extraordinary embroidery arrangements. The panel designs are simplified forms of arrows, chevrons and squash blossoms. The attention to detail in the design approaches true artful expression.

As evidence by their product, Wide Ruins

weavers practice their craft with the utmost diligence, always striving for quality construction and continually searching for the yet-undiscovered tinge that might lie in the dye-bath of a wild plum or juniper seed.

In some quarters, a division of Wide Ruins rugs is made. At the post of Pine Springs, located 10 miles east in the timbered slopes of the Defiance Plateau, weavers produce excellent fabrics that some buyers call a "Pine Springs." The argument is based on color: that the "Pine Springs" rug utilizes more tones of green, where the Wide Ruins covers a broad spectrum of colors. In the many examples viewed, there is a tendency for the color green to appear in threads from Pine Springs area weaving. This might be explained by the forest setting of the post influencing weavers in their mountain greenery locale. This does not provide a suitable distinction, however, to warrant a separate regional style.

More recently, area weavers in the southern part of the region have introduced to the

Plate 26. Wide Ruins

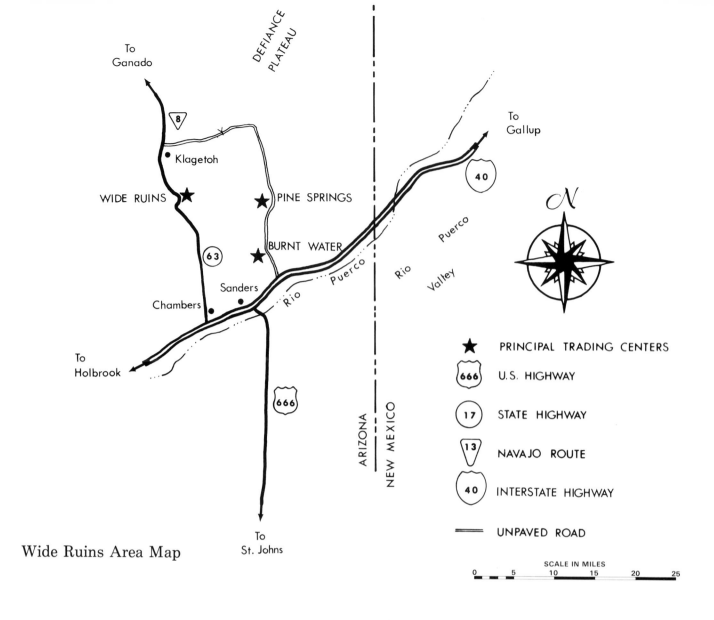

Wide Ruins Area Map

To Ganado

To Gallup

DEFIANCE PLATEAU

Klagetoh

WIDE RUINS

PINE SPRINGS

BURNT WATER

Sanders

Chambers

Rio Puerco

Rio Puerco Valley

To Holbrook

ARIZONA

NEW MEXICO

To St. Johns

★ PRINCIPAL TRADING CENTERS

666 U.S. HIGHWAY

17 STATE HIGHWAY

13 NAVAJO ROUTE

40 INTERSTATE HIGHWAY

═══ UNPAVED ROAD

SCALE IN MILES
0   5   10   15   20   25

Wide Ruins Designs.

Horizontally paneled
with alternating designs

Inter-stitching on solid panels
is common

Crystal "wavy line"
technique

Solid color panels
(usually outlined in another color)

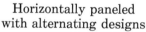

Hatch work

Beading techniques

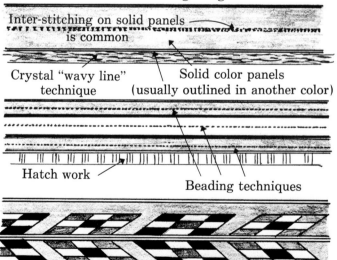

Stylized arrows for chevrons

Multiple squash blossoms

Borderless

market a rug called the "Burnt Water." As beautifully depicted in *Arizona Highways* Magazine (July, 1974), this rug type could possibly merit regional recognition if production continues. The rug features primarily the vegetal earth tones of the Wide Ruins. In overall motif, however, the similarity ends. The designs are highly complex outlines of serrated diamonds, triangles and boxes that are suggestive of stylized Ganado designs. The so-called "Burnt Water" is usually boldly bordered, sometimes exhibiting multiple inner borders. In the examples studied, two incorporated Wide Ruins characteristics of horizontal stripes and bands as end panels. The weave appears excellent and beautifully balanced in pattern. The traditional Navajo designs of the rug, coupled with predominantly golden pastel hues, could provide an exciting new example for contemporary buyers, particularly in light of its recent publicity.

WEAVING AREA

Trading Post

Burnt Water Trading Post
Pine Springs Trading Post
Wide Ruins Trading Post (Pop. 1,015)

Traders

E. Brady Smithson
Norman Ashcroft
Mr. and Mrs. John Rieffer

WEAVERS

Marie Ashley
Mary J. Barker
Marie L. Billey
Annie H. Bonnie
Mabel Burnside
Marie Burnside
Blanche Hale

Mary N. Hale
Mary G. Johnson
Eunice F. Lee
Fanny Lee
Mary Chee Lee
Mary C. Nez
Nellie Roan
Eleanor Roanhorse

Mary Silversmith
Agnes Smith
Ellen Smith
Marjorie Spencer
Lottie Thompson
Annie F. Tsosie
Anita Wilson

COMPARATIVE COSTS
(Range: $20-$150 per Square Foot)

Year	3 x 5	4 x 6	6 x 9	Large Specials
1964	$ 50-200	$200-300	$ 300-500	$ 600 & Up
1974	$300-600	$750-1000	$1000-1500	$2000 & Up

Tonalea (Red Lake Trading Post) — on the Rainbow Trail

Western Reservation
(Tonalea)

Chapter 11

Red Lake Trading Post

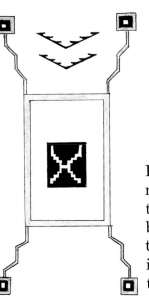

Elevation: 6457'
Post Office Established:
     1926
Trader: Jerry   Norris
Owner: Babbitt Brothers
     Company

THE POST

The Red Lake Trading Post at Tonalea, Navajo meaning "where water comes together", is said to be the birthplace of the Reservation's most controversial and interestingly designed rug — the Storm Pattern.

Situated halfway down the slope of a sandy mesa, with environs strongly resembling a desert of the Far East, the trading post is named for a shallow expanse of land that is only a "lake" during wet years. The best thing about Red Lake, and it

is argumentive, is the view to the east where Black Mesa breaks the rather desolate, unattractive foreground. Rattlesnakes thrived and love the place. Trader Johnny O'Farrell (1918-1935) killed them by the hordes during spring and summer months. Johnny's wife, Cora, gained more than a regional reputation for serving the meat to passers by. *"Many a traveler gagged a bit after eating a delicious tuna sandwich when told that it was freshly killed and boiled rattlesnake meat."*[34] Equally interesting was Cora's "squash blossom" — a threaded necklace of a rattlesnake's spinal column.

Red Lake Trading Post was established in 1881, in the northwest corner of the Hopi Reservation, by Joseph H. Lee, son of John Doyle Lee of Lee's Ferry fame. The post was situated at two different sites prior to its present location. Lee's original store, a canvas-topped shack, was two miles down the wash to the southwest. In 1885 George McAdams

Red Lake Trading Post before improved roads, circa 1949.
(Jack Snow photo, courtesy: Photograph Collection, Museum of New Mexico).

moved the store back to the east, almost directly across the lake from the present trading post. In 1888, McAdams sold out to a Dutchman named Dittenhoffer. "Ditt," as he was called, was killed in a lover's quarrel at the post in 1890. His principal creditor, Charles Babbitt of Babbitt Brothers Trading Company of Flagstaff, assumed active control of the post a year later, and moved the operation to its present rock-constructed, two-story quarters in 1891.

The post remains to this day as a company operated enterprise. Babbitt Brothers, who own and control a chain of trading posts on the Navajo and Hopi Reservations, initiate their business through a resident manager-trader arrangement with partnership privileges. Beginning in 1891, with a first manager named Sam Preston, the succession of employees have been: H. K. Warren (1897-1905), Earl Boyer (1905-1918), Johnny O'-Farrell (1918-1935), Floyd Boyle (1935-1953), Coit Patterson (1953-1955), Harold Lockhart (1955-1973).[35] Jerry Norris, the present trader, assumed managership of the store in late 1973.

One of the more interesting sidelights to the old post were the periodic visits of the noted author, Zane Grey. Grey, seemingly quite taken with the northwest corner of the Indian country, was the guest of trader Earl Boyer on several occasions between 1911-1914 while gathering material for the *Rainbow Trail* (1915). The first chapter of the book is set at Red Lake Trading Post.

THE RUG

The basic design of the Storm Pattern is a bordered rug that is highly symmetrical, displaying certain standard features. Always there is a square or rectangular center from which radiating lines lead to the four corners, where additional squares are set. Secondary elements may include zigzags, diamonds, swastikas, arrows, and stepped terraces serving as fillers along the borders. The rug tends to be elongated in shape to facilitate connecting lines between the rectangular designs. Weavers of the Storm Pattern work primarily in red-black-gray-white combinations with some brightly colored anilines gaining in popularity.

The contemporary Storm Pattern, although still very much in evidence in western sectors, is now being found all over the Reservation. Beautiful examples are reflected in some areas and usually display characteristics of the local regional style. Even vegetal-dyed Storms are beginning to appear on racks.

The origin of the Storm Pattern has prompted considerable debate. The general inclination is to consider it symbolic, although the symbolism appears to have been conceived by a white man. The traditional sales factor in describing the alleged "sacredness" of the rug is that the center square is the hogan, or "center of the world," and that the four squares at each of the corners represent the four sacred mountains of Navajo mythology.[36] The connecting lines, usually zigzagged, are intended as lightning bolts carrying blessings to and fro between the squares, thus bestowing good spirits on the weaver and her household.

Some writers credit an early trader at Tonalea with devising the Storm Pattern. Others say that it is a variation of a commercial design that appeared on flour sacks being shipped out of Flagstaff at the turn of the century. In *Navajo Trading Days*, Elizabeth Hegemann portrays a rug that displays all of the standard features of a contemporary Storm Pattern. Her caption reads, "*A typical and popular rug pattern woven in the district of Western Navajo between Kayenta and Tuba. Many of the good weavers of the Tsay-utcissi family used this design of the Four Mountains bordering the Navajo World with the lake in the middle, and the Sacred Arrows, and Whirling Logs. This was called the Red Lake pattern because a trader at that post had originated the design sometime after 1900.*"[37] Another possibility would seem to rest with the imaginative brain of John B. Moore of Crystal. Moore was continually involved with design innovations; pictured in his mail order catalog, *The Navajo* (1911), is a perfect example of a modern-day Storm Pattern. Moore called this his ER-20 Class, "special design rug" and noted that it is legendary in Navajo mythology and not many weavers will do it for superstitious reasons. Considering that passage, it would appear that Mr. Moore's design abilities were possibly exceeded by his salesmanship.

Storm Pattern

PLATE XXVIII

Special Design and Weave by "Dug-gau-eth-lun bi Dazhie."

From "ER-20" class, original 64x92 inches in size. This pattern is one of the really legendary designs embodying a portion of the Navajo mythology. Not many weavers will do it for superstitious reasons and on that account its production is practically confined to one family or clan. It is an improved adaptation of Plate IX, also originated by this same woman, and done in red, white and black. She, and her immediate relatives, have been making it as shown here for two or three years past, and the rug has never failed to satisfy when shown to a prospective buyer. The trouble has been to get enough of them made, and to overcome this is the main purpose of this engraving. With the pattern for a working model, we hope to get other weavers to making it.

"ER-20" class, size 45x75 inches up to 6x9 feet and price, 90c to $1.00 per square foot, or $21.00 to $23.50 for small, and up or down, according to size. Made to order in any size and colors desired at price in proportion to size, but the colors shown can hardly be improved upon.

Very rarely done in the "T-XX" class, but at $1.00 to $2.00 per lb., if we should chance to have any. Not made to order in this class.

John B. Moore's special design rug, a forerunner to the modern Storm Pattern.

(Reprinted from *The Navajo*, 1911, courtesy: Gallup, New Mexico, Public Library).

Plate 28. Storm Pattern

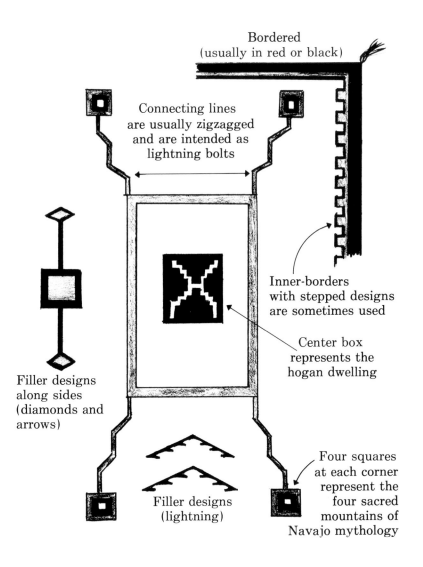

Bordered
(usually in red or black)

Connecting lines
are usually zigzagged
and are intended as
lightning bolts

Inner-borders
with stepped designs
are sometimes used

Center box
represents the
hogan dwelling

Filler designs
along sides
(diamonds and
arrows)

Filler designs
(lightning)

Four squares
at each corner
represent the
four sacred
mountains of
Navajo mythology

Storm Pattern Designs

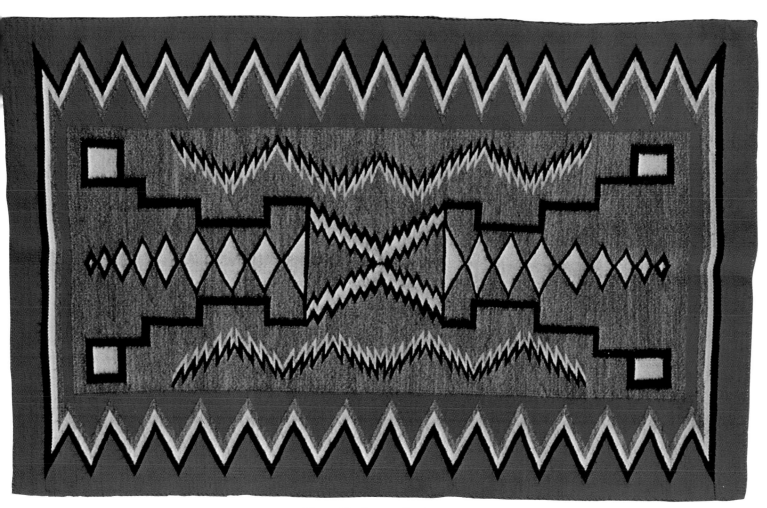

Plate 29. Storm Pattern

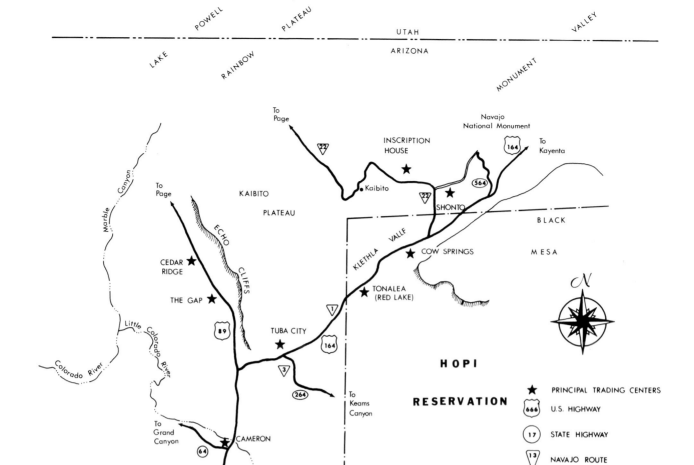

Western Reservation Area Map

WEAVING AREA

Trading Posts

Cameron Trading Post (Pop. 1,402)
Cedar Ridge Trading Post
Cow Springs Trading Post
Inscription House Trading Post (Pop. 1,217)
Shonto Trading Post (Pop. 1,535)
The Gap Trading Post
Red Lake Trading Post (Tonalea, Pop. 2,098)
Tuba City Trading Post (Pop. 2,230)

Traders

Champ Pitts
Don Norris
Tom Hoit
Stokes Carson
Willima McKinley
Troy Washburn
Jerry Norris
Arlis Corneilson

WEAVERS

Mary Begamble	Curti Daw	Bessie Sellers
Lucille Begay	Bessie Eltsosie	Susie Tacheene
May B. Begay	Mary S. Fowler	Mary Tisi
Veronica Begay	Betty Ann Huskon	Lily Touchin
Lorinda Bennette	Leona Littleman	Lillie Nes Tsosi
Jean Blackhat	Jane Nez	Alice Williams
Mary Clark	Mary S. Nez	

COMPARATIVE COSTS
(Range: $10-$75 per Square Foot)

Year	3 x 5	4 x 6	6 x 9	Large Specials
1964	$40-100	$150-250	$250-350	$500 & Up
1974	$75-150	$250-350	$400-750	$1000 & Up

Specialty Rugs and Other Types

Plate 30. Chief Blanket

Generally of small to moderate size, the modern-day Chief-designed rug is made of aniline-dyed red, black, brown, or dark blue handspun yarn, set in horizontal stripes interspaced with bands of white or gray. Smaller design elements, such as checks, diamonds, and crosses may occupy the center and corner edges. The rug has lost the significance for which it was named. Its design continues to live, however, because of the historical prestige it once enjoyed.

Plate 31. Outline

Usually in the 3 x 5 size range, the Outline rug is constructed of both aniline-dyed, handspun and commercial yarn and features a multiple outlining of the designs in different colors. The rug is usually bordered encasing a large central motif, such as a diamond or square.

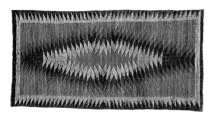

Plate 32. Raised Outline

Developed by the late Ned Hatathli in the 1950's as a Navajo Arts and Craft Guild project, this rug type is one of the latest innovations in contemporary Navajo weaving. It is mostly of aniline-dyed, handspun yarn possessing a border. The patterns are outlined in threads of two alternating colors that are slightly raised to give the design a three-dimensional look. The raised outline appears on but one side, giving the rug type the distinction of having a front and back surface. The project was initiated through a group of weavers on Coal Mine Mesa, southeast of Tuba City. For a number of years, it enjoyed regional style status, but in recent times, the weaving technique has spread throughout the Reservation.

Plate 33. Monogram

Usually square and small in size, the monogram rug can carry almost any message the weaver desires; people's names, places of business, patriotic slogans, etc. Both commercial and aniline-dyed, handspun yarn is used.

Plate 34. Pictorial

Amsden, in discussing pictorial rugs says, *"It is doubtful if any weaver ever attempted to draw a picture to tell a story upon her loom until after the American conquest. Now she launches forth ambitiously with flags and rampant eagles and square-wheeled railway cars."*[38]

As early as the late 1800's, Navajo weavers illustrated their textiles with pictures of animals and human forms. The pictorial rug of today is woven in a variety of usually bright commercial yarn and aniline-dyed colors. Likewise, a variety of subject matter is displayed depending upon the fancy of the weaver: pickup trucks, hogans, mountains, animals (particularly horses, cattle, and sheep), and people can all occupy space in a somewhat crowded manner. A favorite pictorial presentation that has endured from early day graphics to the present is a large, leafless tree with arrays of multiple-colored birds perched upon the branches. The pictorial is generally in the small to moderate range in size and usually without a border.

Plate 35. Monogram-Pictorial

Combining words with pictures on a rug is a relatively modern approach. An American flag with U.S.A. across the top, the name of a person, or the name of a trading post above a building all add personal touches to a rug that often conveys more meaning to whom it is directed, rather than general appeal. Small sizes are prevalent, with both commercial yarn and aniline dyes utilized.

Plate 36. Hide Rug

A rather rare specialty of moderate size that depicts the skinned rawhide of a cow. An imaginative piece that is woven with commercial yarn, clearly outlines the reddish-brown body (complete with tail) and white markings of a spread hide. Some examples are expertly done and from distant viewing remarkably resemble a skin surface.

Plate 37. Circular

Another innovation that has emerged is a small rug which surfaced in 1971. Completely circular (18" in circumference), it is woven in typical Ganado designs with characteristic aniline red-black-gray-white colors. An air of intrigue surrounds the rug inasmuch as the weavers who accomplish this feat refuse to allow anyone to observe their technique or examine their loom.

Plate 38. Sandpainting

These rugs are woven copies, though not exact, of sandpainting designs. The rugs are unbordered, small and square in size (3' x 3', 5' x 5'). They are light-weight and composed of both commercial and aniline-dyed, handspun yarn. Backgrounds are usually tan with brighter, multiple colors composing the designs. The overall depictions, taken from actual sacred healing designs, are quite busy and intricate. The favorite subjects in modern-day rugs are the sandpaintings of the Whirling Log, Shooting Chant, Water Creatures, and the Earth Creatures.

Plate 39. Tufted

An unusual rug not too often found in contemporary weaving is the tufted weave — the second front and back side in a Navajo fabric. In essence, it is a shag-type rug accomplished by inserting long strands of Angora goat wool along with the weft threads. It is of small and irregular size.

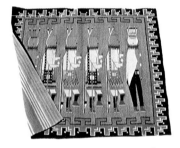

Plate 40. Two-Faced

A difficult rug, the Two-Faced is actually a fabric piece in which the two sides display entirely different designs and colors. To achieve this, the weaver places the weft threads one behind the other, instead of the conventional placement with one thread placed atop the other. The rug is rare and understandably expensive. Being doubled in thickness in a two-styles-in-one development, it is more often coarse-textured and heavy. The Two-Faced rug dates from the late 1880's. It has never been extremely popular, but because of its unique and novel construction, is attractive for collectors. Handspun yarn of both aniline and vegetal dyes are primarily used.

Plate 41. Diamond Twill

Plate 42. Braided Twill

The term "twill" not only signifies a rug type but also a style of weaving that is achieved through arrangement of the loom heddles. Amsden explains, *"Twilling is a constant diagonal progression of stitches produced by the regular alteration of the point of insertion of warp and weft. The plain weave, for example, uses but two sheds, permitting no alternation of this point; the result is a fabric of vertical ribs with one string of warp (commonly) as the core of each. Twilling on the other hand (as done by the Navajo), employs four sheds, controlled by three heddles and the shed rod, the heddle arrangement being calculated to throw each stitch of weft one warp string to the right or left of the one preceeding it. The result is a fabric of diagonal rather than vertical ribs."*[39] Basically, there are three types of twill designs: (1) diamond twill, (2) braided (herringbone or diagonal) twill, and (3) the double weave.[40]

Plate 43. Double Weave

The term double weave as applied to twilling is a misnomer. The name incorrectly refers to a braided twill (or combination of braided twill alternating with a diamond twill) and has the order of colors reversed on the two sides. The pattern remains identical, but by alternating colors through the entire width of the sheds, the arrangement of color changes from one side to the other.

In the twill types, there is no specific usage of yarn or dyes. Colors range from vegetal pastels to bright anilines.

Plate 44. Woman's Dress

This fabric is actually not a rug, but represents still another example of a specialty type weave. The style of the Woman's Dress dates from the earliest influences of Pueblo women on the Navajo mode of attire. Design of the Navajo Woman's Dress is different from the plain Pueblo style, in that the Puebloans utilized one piece that was of sufficient width to permit doubling. The Navajo Woman's Dress consists of two pieces of identical size and shape to be worn as front and back pieces. It is secured at top and bottom, with long slits prevailing on the sides to allow for arm movement. There are no sleeves. Simple stripes and small design elements decorated the piece in colors of black, red, and blue.

The Woman's Dress of today still retains the basic early style and design of the past century. It is constructed usually of handspun yarn in colors of deep aniline red, black, and blue.

Three large panels, with alternating blocks of color, comprise the overall presentation, with smaller stripes and bands interspaced between. Small geometrics, such as rows of diamonds or checks, usually decorate the top and bottom sections.

A smaller version of the Woman's Dress, appropriately called Child's Dress, occasionally finds its way to rug outlets. These are quite rare and are sought as collectors' items.

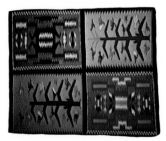

Plate 45. Four-In-One

Perhaps the rarest rug in contemporary Navajo weaving is the Four-In-One style. It consists of either aniline-dyed, handspun, or commercial yarn woven into an overall bordered format consisting of four equal quadrants. Each square contains a separate design, each different from the other three. Some Four-In-One rugs display pairs of squares, i.e. two Sandpaintings and two Pictorials.

These rugs require a great deal of imagination, talent, and perseverance. They are rarely attempted, and highly prized.

OTHER RUG TYPES

Plate 46. Saddle Blanket

The Saddle Blanket is the only Navajo textile woven today that the Indians use for a functional purpose. It comes in two sizes: single (30" x 30") and double (30" x 60"). The blanket is often purposely coarse-woven (to take hard wear beneath the saddle) of aniline-dyed, handspun yarn. The piece is usually unbordered, featuring simple serration and stripe and band designs. Colors are mostly bright, particularly at the corners and ends. Tassels are incorporated at the four corners, in the more elaborate pieces. Twill weaving is used quite often in developing Saddle Blanket styles. Many people use the Saddle Blanket as a floor piece, mainly because of its durability and colorful fibers.

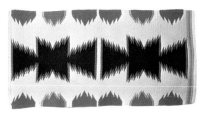

Plate 47. Double Saddle Blanket

Referred to by some writers as a regional style rug, the Gallup Throw is actually a tourist-curio item developed near Gallup for the railroad passengers. Today it can be found woven in many places on the Reservation.

Some novice weavers practice with the throw-type rug before attempting more difficult designs and weaves. It is a small, inexpensive, borderless runner or table-top piece, often possessing a cotton warp, which is usually left dangling as a one or two inch fringe on one end. The rug is commonly of bright, handspun, aniline-dyed yarn. Designs are relatively simple; broad chevrons, stripes, stylized diamonds, and some with displays of the Yei figure.

Plate 48. Gallup Throw

A fabric of almost any dimension; poor to excellent weave; featuring handspun or commercial yarn; aniline-dyed or vegetal-dyes; incorporating a multitude of designs; bordered or borderless. It may be woven in any locale on the Reservation. The distinction of the general rug is that it does not possess sufficient characteristics of either a regional style rug or a specialty rug.

Plate 49. General Rug

Maxwell (1963) may have been a perfectionist when he suggested that anybody requiring a made-to-order rug should either learn to weave or marry a weaver! True, a definite communication problem exists between the weaver and the customer who wishes to own a precisely ordered type of rug. What may start out to be an understanding of size, color, dye, and style invariably changes as the rug develops. Most weavers sell their craft through their area trader, and he is, understandably so, the only non-Indian who can suggest, influence, or commission for a certain type rug. The price for special order rugs is usually quite high and the results almost always uncertain. Acquaintances made with traders, weavers, retailers, etc. on the Reservation can sometimes result in getting just what you ordered (see Plates 9 and 19).

CORRELATION CHART OF REGIONAL STYLE WEAVING CENTERS:

James (1974)	Tanner (1968)	Bahti (1966)
1. Shiprock	1. Farmington-Shiprock	1. Shiprock-Lukachukai
2. Lukachukai	2. Lukachukai-Greasewood	
3. Teec Nos Pos	3. Teec Nos Pos	2. Teec Nos Pos
4. Crystal	4. Crystal	3. Crystal
5. Two Gray Hills	5. Two Gray Hills	4. Two Gray Hills
6. Chinle	6. Chinle	5. Chinle
		6. Nazlini
7. Ganado	7. Ganado	7. Ganado
	8. Kayenta	8. Klagetoh
8. Wide Ruins	9. Wide Ruins - Pine Springs	9. Wide Ruins
9. Western Reservation	10. Western Reservation	10. Western Reservation
	11. Gallup	11. Gallup
	12. Coal Mine Mesa	12. Coal Mine Mesa

Dutton (1963)	Maxwell (1963)	Kent (1961)
San Juan	1. Shiprock	1. Shiprock
Round Rock	2. Lukachukai	2. Lukachukai
Teec Nos Pos	3. Teec Nos Pos 4. Red Mesa	3. Teec Nos Pos
Crystal	5. Crystal	4. Crystal
Two Gray Hills Tocito Burnham	6. Two Gray Hills	5. Two Gray Hills
Chinle Black Mountain Nazlini	7. Chinle	6. Chinle
Ganado Kayenta Rock Point Steamboat	8. Ganado 9. Keams Canyon — Piñon	7. Ganado 8. Keams Canyon
Wide Ruins	10. Wide Ruins	9. Wide Ruins
Western Reservation	11. Western Reservation	10. Western Reservation
Gallup	12. Gallup	
	13. Coal Mine Mesa	11. Coal Mine Mesa
Off-Reservation (Ramah-Alamo-Canoncito)		12. Coppermine
		13. Shonto-Navajo Mountain

Appendix I

Rules in Buying a Navajo Rug

Not all Navajo rugs are examples of quality craftsmanship. Consider the following when making a purchase.

(1) **Remember,** a Navajo rug is not 100 percent perfect; if it were, it would be like a machine-made piece and thus lose the charm of being handmade. Small flaws are acceptable only if they don't detract from the overall presentation of the fabric.

(2) **Always** open the rug, full width and length. Smooth out all the wrinkles and corners. The rug should not curl up and should be even in form. Look at both sides, get the full visual impact of the design.

(3) **Check** the weave. Is it tight? Is the design uniform and even from one end to the other? The ends and borders should be straight and the corners properly tied off. Make sure there are no warp threads exposed.

(4) **Feel** the smoothness of the rug. Is the wool textured the same throughout the fabric? Watch for heavy lumping; likewise, thinly spaced areas.

(5) With a keen eye, **watch** for color uniformity. Since only a small amount of yarn can be dyed at a time, a weaver may become careless with her dyebath and variations may emerge. In the natural white tones, watch for dirty gray casts, as well as streaks of other cardings. Also whitening agents, such as powder and chalk, may be used to conceal dirty yarn.

(6) **Consider** the overall motif. Does it fulfill your purpose of purchase? Will it fit into your scheme of home decorating? Will it hang on the wall, or be placed on the floor?

(7) If the appeal is esthetically right, the size is right, and the price is right — **buy it!** Fine Navajo rugs are a good investment. The turnover is high and the choice fabrics do not linger long on the racks. The one you had your eye on today may be gone tomorrow.

(8) **Consult** and buy from quality dealers. Outlets with good reputations cannot afford to deal in rugs with the unfavorable characteristics and practices outlined here.

(9) **Beware** of Mexican imitations. Excellent replica copies of Navajo designs can be easily mistaken by unsuspecting buyers. The principal keys in recognizing a Mexican rug are: (1) examine for multiple warps along the sides, (2) knotted warps along the top and bottom, and (3) a coarse, loosely-woven product. Exercise caution with seemingly "good deal" prices.

Appendix II

Care of a Navajo Rug

(1) When rugs are placed on the floor, **use** a foam mat beneath.

(2) **Rotate** the sides of the rug and reverse the ends occasionally. This will allow for uniform wear and mellowing of colors. When hung on a wall, a rug is usually in more direct sunlight, and rotations should be more frequent.

(3) Normal vacuum cleaning is sufficient. **Never** "shake out" a Navajo rug; the snapping action may loosen the end cords, causing warp and weft threads to unravel.

(4) **Never** wash the rug. If small spots occur, commercial removers will usually suffice. If a major cleaning is necessary, consult a reputable rug dealer for recommendation of a dry cleaner who specializes in rug care.

(5) If water is spilled on a rug, blot it **immediately** to minimize the running of colors. Improperly set colorants (both vegetal and commercial), when combined with water can literally destroy the visual portrait of a rug. The color red is the hardest to neutralize.

(6) Navajo rugs should **always** be de-mothed, whether they are in use or not. In wall hangings, remember to treat both sides.

(7) If a rug is to be stored for an indefinite period, always **roll** it; folding may cause crimping of the threads, resulting in permanent creases. Cedar-lined chests are recommended as safe, suitable storage containers.

(8) In some rugs, a minor curling effect may occur along the ends and corners. **Simply** untie the end cords, gently smooth out the curled surface, and retie the tassels.

Appendix III

1974 Navajo Weaving Awards

1. New Mexico State Fair
2. Navajo Nation Fair
3. Gallup Ceremonial
4. Scottsdale National Indian
   Arts Council

1974 NEW MEXICO STATE FAIR

Type of Rug	Blue Ribbon - 1st Place
Aniline Dye Rug	Susie E. Curtis, Window Rock, Ariz.
Natural Wool Rug	Desbah Evans, Window Rock, Ariz.
Vegetal Dye Rug	Mary Yellowhorse, Sanders, Ariz.
Vegetal Dye Rug (Tapestry)	Minnie Begay, Ganado, Ariz.
Two Gray Hills Rug	Stella Curley, Two Gray Hills, N. Mex.
Two Gray Hills (Tapestry)	Sailen Hale, Fruitland, N. Mex.
Yei Figure Rug (any size)	Lilly Chee, Waterflow, N. Mex.
Yei Rug (Tapestry)	Nellie Churlene, Waterflow, N. Mex.
Yei Figure Rug—Commercial Yarn (any size)	Annie Blue Eyes, Waterflow, N. Mex.
Rug—Commercial Yarn (any size)	Hazel Taylor, Teec Nos Pos, Ariz.
Rug (any type with borders)	Winnie Becenti, Window Rock, Ariz.
Rug (Two-Faced, any type)	Mary Jones, Crownpoint, N. Mex.
Rug (Sandpainting, any type)	Daisy Buston, Shiprock, N. Mex.
Rug (any type, larger than 8' x 10')	Mary Hoskie, Piñon, Ariz.
Rug (any type, smaller than 2' x 3')	Sarah Begay, Tohatchi, N. Mex.
Pictorial Rug	Sarah Benally, Waterflow, N. Mex.
Rug (other than mentioned)	Monitta James, Lukachukai, Ariz.
Commercial Yarn (Tapestry)	Sarah Begay, Tohatchi, N. Mex.

Type of Rug	Red Ribbon - 2nd Place
Aniline Dye Rug	Marie Begay, Window Rock, Ariz.
Natural Wool Rug	Nora Tsosie Johnson, Window Rock, Ariz.
Vegetal Dye Rug	Mary Nez Hale, Sanders, Ariz.
Vegetal Dye Rug (Tapestry)	Ellen Smith, Albuquerque, N. Mex.
Two Gray Hills Rug	Rachel Curley, Albuquerque, N. Mex.
Two Gray Hills (Tapestry)	Rachelle Curley, Cuba, N. Mex.
Yei Figure Rug (any size)	Cecila McKinley, Waterflow, N. Mex.
Yei Rug (Tapestry)	Josie Begay, Gallup, N. Mex.
Yei Figure Rug—Commercial Yarn (any size)	Lena George, Waterflow, N. Mex.
Rug—Commercial Yarn (any size)	Sally Scott, Teec Nos Pos, Ariz.
Rug (any type with borders)	Lola Hosteen, Piñon, Ariz.
Rug (any type, larger than 8′ x 10′)	Louise Slim, Piñon, Ariz.
Rug (any type, smaller than 2′ x 3′)	Agnes Smith, Albuquerque, N. Mex.
Pictorial Rug	I. Moran, Chinle, Ariz.
Rug (other than mentioned)	M. E. Nez, Teec Nos Pos, Ariz.
Commercial Yarn (Tapestry)	Sarah Begay, Tohatchi, N. Mex.

Type of Rug	White Ribbon - 3rd Place
Aniline Dye Rug	Elizabeth George, Ganado, Ariz.
Natural Wool Rug	Elizabeth Belon, Window Rock, Ariz.
Vegetal Dye Rug	Mary Nez Hale, Sanders, Ariz.
Vegetal Dye Rug (Tapestry)	Eleanor Nelson, Sanders, Ariz.
Two Gray Hills Rug	Alice Begay, Window Rock, Ariz.
Two Gray Hills (Tapestry)	Dorene Gould, Fruitland, N. Mex.
Yei Figure Rug (any size)	Phyllis Benally, Fruitland, N. Mex.
Yei Rug (Tapestry)	Rose Bia, Window Rock, Ariz.
Yei Figure Rug—Commercial Yarn (any size)	M. Gorman, Lukachukai, Ariz.
Rug—Commercial Yarn (any size)	Dora Lee, Teec Nos Pos, Ariz.
Rug (any type with borders)	Mary Charlie, Albuquerque, N. Mex.
Rug (Sandpainting, any type)	Lucy Sims, Gallup, N. Mex.
Rug (any type, larger than 8′ x 10′)	Martha Judd, Piñon, Ariz.
Rug (any type, smaller than 2′ x 3′)	Sadie Lee, Waterflow, N. Mex.
Pictorial Rug	T. Yellowhair, Gallup, N. Mex.
Rug (other than mentioned)	Desbah Evans, Window Rock, Ariz.
Commercial Yarn (Tapestry)	Sarah Begay, Tohatchi, N. Mex.

Best Rug in Show
Sailene Dale, Fruitland, N. Mex.

NAVAJO NATION FAIR

Blue Ribbon - 1st Place	Type of Rug
Mary J. James*	Vegetal Dye Rug
Nora Tsosie Johnson**	Two Gray Hills, Tapestry
Mary Martin	Natural Wool Rug
Rose Tracy	Yei Figure Rug, Commercial Yarn
Rose Bia	Yei Figure, Tapestry
Eleanor Roanhorse	Vegetal Dye Rug, Tapestry
Winnie Becenti	Aniline Dye Rug
Annie James Taliman	Two-Face Rug (any type)
Karen W. Yazzie	Pictorial Rug
Bertha Shaw	Chief Blanket
Susie Bia	Yei Figure Rug (any size)

Red Ribbon - 2nd Place	Type of Rug
Mary Johnson	Chief Blanket
Desbah Evans	Pictorial Rug
Elizabeth Belone	Two Gray Hills Rug
Eunice Lee	Vegetal Dye Rug, Tapestry
Janet Thompson	Aniline Dye Rug
Desbah Evans	Natural Wool Rug
Susie Bia	Yei Figure Rug (any size)
Desbah Evans	Vegetal Dye Rug
Sadie B. Curtis	Yei Figure Rug, Commercial Yarn (any size)

White Ribbon - 3rd Place	Type of Rug
Eleanor Denetso	Yei Figure, Commercial Yarn (any size)
Mary D. Nez	Vegetal Dye Rug
Lena Hubbard	Natural Wool Rug
Winnie Becenti	Aniline Dye Rug
Desbah Evans	Pictorial Rug

*Grand Prize Award
**Special Judges Award

INTER-TRIBAL
INDIAN
CEREMONIAL

GALLUP NEW MEXICO
THE INDIAN CAPITAL

1974 GALLUP CEREMONIAL

Blue Ribbon - 1st Place	Type of Rug
1. Alice Begay	Aniline Rug (with border)
6. Alice Begay	Navajo Rug
11. Ellen Smith	Navajo Rug
13. Linette Nez	Tapestry Rug
	Best in its Class Central M. Co.
15. Margaret Tom	Chief
16. Lillian Whitesheep	Pictorial
19. Jean Blackhat	Storm Pattern
23. Eunice Wilson	Two-Faced
24. Mary Long	Weaving Innovation
27. Marilyn Yazzie	Yei Fox Dancer (Germantown)
29. Marie Wallace	Teec Nos Pos
31. Eileen Reed	Diamond Weave
35. Mary E. Lee	Aniline Dye (with border)
41. Elizibeth Goodman	Raised Outline
45. Andrey Wilson	Two-Faced Rug
48. Mrs. Harrison	Single Saddle Blanket
49. Mary E. Lee	Vegetal Dye (with border)
50. Betty Bia	Fox Dancer
51. Lula Be Brown	Fox Dancer
52. Susie Bia	Vegetal Dye (with border)
54. Martha Johnson	Vegetal Dye (without border)
55. Betty Bia	Aniline Dye (without border)
59. Phyllis Benally	Vegetal Dye Yei (over 12')
60. Jeanita Naher	Crystal (15/40')
62. Anna Falk	Crystal (15/40')
64. Josephine Curley	Double Saddle Blanket
65. Ruby Manuelito	Sandpainting
68. Mae Bedah	Yei (Natural)
73. Barbara Etsitty	Raised Outline
74. Fannie Benally	Pictorial
75. Ruby Payer	Two-Faced Rug
76. Marilyn Atcitty	Aniline Dye (without border)
77. Susie Scott	Natural Wool (without border)
79. Agnes Bia	Crystal
80. Flora Roanhorse	Vegetal Dye
81. Betty Wilson	Two Gray Hills
82. Agnes Johnson	Aniline Dye (with border)

| 83. Roslyn Begay | Teec Nos Pos |
| 85. Herbert Tohamptewa | Sash |

Red Ribbon - 2nd Place	**Type of Rug**
2. Mary Etsitty	Storm Pattern
4. Ella Begay	Navajo Rug
8. Nellie N. Lee	Navajo Rug
12. Mary Lee Gould	Tapestry Rug
17. Elizibeth Goodman	Raised Outline
21. Fanny Hoskie	Two Gray Hills
22. Grace Todachine	Two-Faced
25. Elizibeth Goodman	Weaving Innovation
28. Daisy Peshlakeii	Yei Fox Dancer (Germantown)
30. Connie Hat	Teec Nos Pos
33. Mary Reid	Aniline Dye (without border)
36. Winnie James	Vegetal Dye (with border)
37. Mary Beth Moore	Vegetal Dye (without border)
39. Faye C. George	Mohair Rug
42. Mae Simpson	Storm Pattern
44. Rosetti Davis Brown	Two-Faced Rug
53. Ellowise Bia	Vegetal Dye (without border)
56. Katherine Lee	Aniline Dye (without border 15/40')
57. Helen Tso	Aniline (with border)
58. Virginia Ambrose	Vegetal Dye (without border 15/40')
63. Hazel Peyer	Machine Processed
66. Sarah Zahs	Two Gray Hills
69. Sarah Benally	Fox Dancer (Natural Wool)
71. Cecilia Willie	Sandpainting (Germantown)
84. Herbert Tohamptewa	Sash

White Ribbon - 3rd Place	**Type of Rug**
3. Mary Goodman	Storm Pattern
5. Mary Reid	Navajo Rug
7. Mary Reid	Navajo Rug
9. Dorothy Mike	Navajo Rug
10. Gladys Belente	Navajo Rug
14. Ason Lia	Aniline Dye
18. Elizabeth Goodman	Raised Outline
20. Fanny Hoskie	Two Gray Hills
26. Maker Unknown	Vegetal Dye Fox Dancer
32. Mary Rose Benally	Storm Pattern
34. Rafels Mather	Aniline Dye (with border)
38. May Navajo	Vegetal Dye (without border)
40. Fannie Farnish	Pictorial
43. Mary Tsosie	Storm Pattern
46. Mary Bah	Vegetal Dye Yei
47. Gee Bah Lee	Twilled Diagonal
61. Ella Rose Perry	Crystal (15/40')
67. Ruby Manuelito	Two Gray Hills
70. Mary Marshall	Sandpainting (Germantown)
72. Julia Peshlakai	Fox Dancer (Germantown)
78. Carline John	Single Saddle Blanket

1-3   Navaho Crafts, P. O. Box 66, Window Rock, Arizona

4-13 Woodard's Indian Arts, 224 W. Coal Ave., Gallup,
      N. Mex.

14-31 Gallup Indian Trading Co., Gallup, N. Mex. 87301

32-53 Tanner's Indian Arts, Box 97, Gallup, N. Mex. 87301

54-83 Russell Foutz Indian Room, 301 W. Main, Farmington,
      N. Mex.

84-85 Balcomb's Indian Arts, Box 410, Taos, N. Mex. 87571

SPECIAL AWARDS

Class 2

Citizens Bank of Gallup   Best in Class Pueblo Textiles
$100.00 Herbert Tohamptewa

Class 1

Central Motor Company	Best in Class Weaving Navajo	
		$200.00
	Maty E. Lee	$150.00
	Linette Nez	$ 50.00
	Alice Begay	$ 50.00

1974 SCOTTSDALE NATIONAL INDIAN ARTS COUNCIL

1st Place	Type of Rug
Lucy Joe	Yei Rug
Lucille Joe	Wide Ruins Rug
Daisy Taugelchee	Two Gray Hills (Tapestry)

2nd Place	Type of Rug
Betty Bia	Yeibechai Rug
Mary Nez	Crystal Rug
Mildred Natoni	Ganado (Tapestry)

3rd Place	Type of Rug
Ella Mae Begay	Yei Rug
Toable Kaylomie	Double-Face Rug
Priscilla Taugelchee	Ganado (Tapestry)

Honor Mention	Type of Rug
Darlene Benally	Pictorial Rug
Sarah Benally	Yei Rug
Rose Keith	Raised Outline Rug
Bessie Lee	Red Mesa Outline Rug
Dorothy Mike	(no description given)
Kathleen Cleveland	Two Gray Hills (Tapestry)

Appendix IV

Plate Descriptions

Cover	Ganado (36″ x 42″) Weaver unknown; Courtesy Hubbell Trading Post, Ganado, Ariz. All colors: aniline-dyed, handspun.
Plate 1	Shiprock Yei (40″x 40″) Weaver: Bernia Pettygras, Shiprock, N. Mex. Author's collection (1969). Colors: background vegetal; figures aniline; some minor commercial yarn, mostly handspun.
Plate 2	Shiprock Yei (40″ x 40″) Weaver unknown; Courtesy: Covered Wagon, Albuquerque, N. Mex. Colors: commercial yarn; natural white background, mostly handspun.
Plate 3	Shiprock Yeibechai (30″ x 36″) Weaver: Rose Peshlakai, Shiprock, N. Mex. Author's collection (1969). Colors: mostly aniline-dyed with some commercial yarn in figures, mostly handspun.
Plate 4	Lukachukai Yei (36″ x 60″) Weaver unknown. Courtesy: Hubbell Trading Post, Ganado, Ariz. All colors: aniline-dyed, handspun.
Plate 5	Lukachukai Yei (40″ x 40″) Weaver unknown. Courtesy: Hubbell Trading Post, Ganado, Ariz. All colors; aniline-dyed, handspun.
Plate 6	Teec Nos Pos (72″ x 108″) Weaver unknown. Courtesy: Covered Wagon, Albuquerque, N. Mex. All colors: aniline-dyed, handspun.
Plate 7	Teec Nos Pos (31″ x 44″) Weaver: Louise Cattleman, Teec Nos Pos, Ariz. Author's collection (1970). All colors: aniline-dyed, handspun.
Plate 8	Teec Nos Pos (48″ x 72″) Weaver unknown. Courtesy: Covered Wagon, Albuquerque, N. Mex. All colors: aniline-dyed, handspun.
Plate 9	Crystal (36″ x 60″) Weaver: Mary Moore, Crystal, N. Mex. Author's collection (1969). Woven especially for the author to incorporate pre-1940 Crystal hook designs into contemporary panelled pattern. Colors: mostly vegetal-dyed with some natural carded gray in center panels, handspun.
Plate 10	Crystal (36″ x 60″) Weaver: Elsie Ann Yazzie, Crystal, N. Mex. Author's collection (1973). Colors: mostly vegetal-dyed with some natural white wool and carded gray, handspun.

Plate 11	Two Gray Hills (30″ x 46″) Weaver unknown. Courtesy: Price's All Indian Shop, Albuquerque, N. Mex. All colors: natural wool carded blends with aniline-dyed black border, handspun.
Plate 12	Two Gray Hills (33½″ x 52½″) Weaver: Mary Bainbridge, Toadlena, N. Mex. Author's collection (1970). All colors: natural wool carded blends with aniline-dyed black border, handspun.
Plate 13	Two Gray Hills Tapestry (32″ x 48″) Weaver unknown. Courtesy: Covered Wagon, Albuquerque, N. Mex. All colors: natural wool carded blends with aniline-dyed black border, handspun.
Plate 14	Two Gray Hills Tapestry (32″ x 40″) Weaver unknown. Courtesy: Price's All Indian Shop, Albuquerque, N. Mex. All colors: natural wool carded blends with aniline-dyed black border, handspun.
Plate 15	Two Gray Hills Tapestry (24″ x 36″) Weaver unknown. Courtesy: Price's All Indian Shop, Albuquerque, N. Mex. All colors: natural wool carded blends with aniline-dyed black border, handspun.
Plate 16	Two Gray Hills Tapestry (24″ x 36″) Weaver unknown. Courtesy: Price's All Indian Shop, Albuquerque, N. Mex. All colors: natural wool carded blends with aniline-dyed black border, handspun.
Plate 17	Chinle (36″ x 44″) Weaver unknown. Courtesy: Hubbell Trading Post, Ganado, Ariz. Colors: horizontal panels, vegetal; squash blossom designs, aniline; handspun.
Plate 18	Chinle (34″ x 48″) Weaver: Nex Bah Lee, Chinle, Ariz. Author's collection (1972). Colors: mostly vegetal–dyed; aniline–dyed black end panels, handspun.
Plate 19	Ganado (36″ x 44″) unfinished on the loom. Weaver: Louise Begay, Ganado, Ariz. Author's collection (1972). Woven especially for the author under instructions and assistance from Bill Young, Hubbell trader. All colors: aniline-dyed, handspun.
Plate 20	Ganado (34″ x 63″) Weaver: Mary James, Ganado, Ariz. Author's collection (1970). All colors: aniline-dyed, handspun.
Plate 21	Ganado (24½″ x 41½″) Weaver: Zonnie Earl, Cornfields, Ariz. Author's collection (1972). All colors: aniline-dyed, handspun.

Plate 22   Ganado (36″ x 42″) Weaver unknown. Courtesy: Hubbell Trading Post, Ganado, Ariz. All colors: aniline-dyed, handspun.

Plate 23   Ganado (36″ x 42″) Weaver unknown. Courtesy: Hubbell Trading Post, Ganado, Ariz. All colors: aniline-dyed, handspun.

Plate 24   Wide Ruins (21½ ″ x 33½ ″) Weaver unknown. Courtesy: Hubbell Trading Post, Ganado, Ariz. All colors: vegetal-dyed, handspun.

Plate 25   Wide Ruins (24″ x 36″) Weaver unknown. Courtesy: Hubbell Trading Post, Ganado, Ariz. All colors: vegetal-dyed, handspun.

Plate 26   Wide Ruins (28″ x 36″) Weaver unknown. Courtesy Hubbell Trading Post, Ganado, Ariz. All colors: vegetal-dyed, handspun.

Plate 27   Storm Pattern (32″ x 58″) in raised outline form. Weaver unknown: Author's collection (1972). Colors: mostly aniline-dyed with some natural carded gray, handspun.

Plate 28   Storm Pattern (24″ x 36″) Weaver unknown. Courtesy: Price's All Indian Shop, Albuquerque, N. Mex. All colors: vegetal-dyed, handspun.

Plate 29   Storm Pattern (36″ x 48″) Weaver unknown. Courtesy: Hubbell Trading Post, Ganado, Ariz. All colors: aniline-dyed, handspun.

Plate 30   Chief Blanket (36″ x 41″) Weaver unknown. Author's collection (1971). All colors: aniline-dyed, handspun.

Plate 31   Outline Rug (33″ x 46″) Weaver unknown. Author's collection (1971). All colors: aniline-dyed, handspun.

Plate 32   Raised Outline (30″ x 60″) Weaver unknown. Author's collection (1968). All colors: aniline-dyed, handspun.

Plate 33   Monogram (28″ x 30″) Weaver: Helen Brown, Chinle, Ariz. Author's collection (1970). Colors: background natural wool blends; design and monogram aniline, handspun.

Plate 34   Pictorial (36″ x 45″) Weaver unknown. Courtesy: Covered Wagon, Albuquerque, N. Mex. Colors: background, natural wool blends; design aniline; some commercial yarn, mostly handspun.

Plate 35   Monogram-Pictorial (24" x 36") Weaver unknown. Courtesy: Hubbell Trading Post, Ganado, Ariz. Colors: turquoise (aniline); black, white, and gray (natural carded wool); tan (vegetal), handspun.

Plate 36   Hide Rug (24" x 36") Weaver unknown. Courtesy: Hubbell Trading Post, Ganado, Ariz. Colors: commercial yarn.

Plate 37   Circular Rug (20" dia.) in double weave form. Weaver: Rose Owen, Cross Canyon, Ariz. Author's collection (1972). All Colors: aniline-dyed, handspun.

Plate 38   Sandpainting (40" x 40") Shooting Chant design. Weaver unknown. Courtesy: Covered Wagon, Albuquerque, N. Mex. Colors: aniline-dyed; some commercial yarn, mostly handspun.

Plate 39   Tufted Weave (27" x 34") Weaver unknown. Author's collection (1973). All natural wool.

Plate 40   Two-Faced (40" x 48") featuring Yeibechai and Chinle designs. Weaver unknown. Courtesy: Covered Wagon, Albuquerque, N. Mex. Colors: combination vegetal and aniline dyes, handspun.

Plate 41   Diamond Twill (29" x 51") Weaver unknown. Author's collection (1967). All colors: aniline-dyed, handspun.

Plate 42   Braided Twill (25½" x 44½") Weaver: Mary Alice Willie, Fort Defiance, Ariz. Author's collection (1969). All colors: vegetal-dyed, handspun.

Plate 43   Double Weave (25" x 34") Weaver: Susie Dale, Cross Canyon, Ariz. Author's collection (1971). All colors: vegetal-dyed, handspun.

Plate 44   Woman's Dress (36" x 48") Weaver unknown. Courtesy: Hubbell Trading Post, Ganado, Ariz. All colors: aniline-dyed, handspun.

Plate 45   Four-In-One (36" x 42") featuring pairs of Storm Patterns and Pictorials. Weaver: Elsie La Pahu, Monument Valley, Ariz. Courtesy: Covered Wagon, Albuquerque, N. Mex. Colors: aniline-dyed, some commercial yarn, mostly handspun.

Plate 46   Single Saddle Blanket (30" x 30") Weaver unknown. Courtesy: Covered Wagon, Albuquerque, N. Mex. All colors: aniline-dyed with cotton tassels, handspun.

Plate 47   Double Saddle Blanket (30″ x 60″) in double weave
            form. Weaver: Susie Tso, Sawmill, Ariz. Auth-
            or's collection (1971). All colors: aniline-dyed,
            with wool tassels, handspun.

Plate 48   Gallup Throw (18″ x 34″) Weaver unknown. Cour-
            tesy: Covered Wagon, Albuquerque, N. Mex.
            All colors: aniline-dyed with cotton warp, hand-
            spun.

Plate 49   General Rug (36″ x 48″) Weaver unknown. Courte-
            sy: Hubbell Trading Post, Ganado, Ariz. All
            colors: aniline-dyed, handspun.

Notes

(1) Amsden (1934), pp. 235-237.

(2) Navajo weavers had access to bayeta as early as 1804, but only in rare quantity. With the advent of Southwest colonization, the fabric became more obtainable, particularly in the mid-1800's. Amsden (1934 p. 142n) refers to the first half of the 19th century of Navajo weaving as the *bayeta period*.

(3) The period between 1880-1890 became known as the era of the eye-dazzlers.

(4) Though rarely practiced, the first bordered rug dates from 1873, (Amsden, 1934, pl. 82, p. 170).

(5) Some contemporary writers recognized different separations in regional style weaving centers. See Correlation Table.

(6) Matthews (1902), p. 182.

(7) Reference to the color black as a natural wool tone is a misnomer. In most cases, it is dyed further to intensify its balance, because most natural shorn wool is not a true black.

(8) Bryan and Young (1940), p. 9.

(9) *Ibid*, pp. 11-12.

(10) *Ibid*, pp. 19-75.

(11) The preparation of the warp thread is done during the spinning process. In almost all cases the threads are natural wool — the one exception being the prevalent use of cotton warp in the small table-top covers known as the Gallup Throw rug. Tonalea trader, Harold Lockhart, reported to the author in 1972 that some nylon warp was in use in that area.

(12) Amsden (1934), outlined nine types of Navajo weaves; six twill weaves, plain weave, two-faced weave, and double weave. The tapestry technique is employed in all of these types. It is the arrangement of the heddles that produces the variants. The so-called "wedge weave" might be considered the one exception, whereas the basic horizontal attitude of the warp is altered. Though rarely practiced in modern time, the "wedge weave" (called "pulled warp" by Amsden), enjoyed popularity during the 1880's-1890's. The principal approach was the stretching of the warp at oblique angles to allow the weft to conform to desired patterns, which were usually set in diagonal, interlocking zigzags. Some writings referred to this style as the "lighting weave."

(13) Personal communication: (July, 1972), Bill Young, Ganado, Arizona.

(14) Called Needles before 1848.

(15) Personal communication: (March, 1973), Ed Foutz, Shiprock, New Mexico.

(16) Personal communication: (January, 1972), Kenneth Kennedy, Lukachukai, Arizona.

(17) Maxwell (1973).

(18) Simpson (1850), p. 78.

(19) Post Office discontinued, 1914. Mail service now directed through Navajo, New Mexico.

(20) National Archives, Record Group 75, 1884, No. 11520.

(21) McNitt (1962, p. 254n), notes that when Charlie Newcomb began trading at Crystal in 1922, a considerable amount of "Moore wool" was still on hand. The supposition of Newcomb was that the machine processed fiber was milled somewhere in Wisconsin.

(22) Moore (1911), pp. 3-4.

(23) Moore's sudden departure from Crystal was clouded with controversy. A local postal scandal involving welfare supplies, in which he was not personally involved, was embarrassing to the point of prompting his retirement. His reputation untarnished and his contribution to Navajo weaving firmly established, he passed away in Kansas in 1923. Letter communication: (February 3, 1975) Don Jensen, Crystal, New Mexico.

(24) Post Office was called Crozier. Mail service discontinued in 1919 and transferred to Newcomb, New Mexico. In recent years trading residents have received their mail through Tohatchi, New Mexico.

(25) Sometimes spelled Two Grey Hills, particularly during early years of the post.

(26) Carded black and white-gray; carded brown and white-tan and beige.

(27) The greatest Navajo male weaver was medicine-man Hosteen Klah (1867-1937). Residing in the Newcomb area, he specialized in sandpainting tapestries that accompanied his ceremonial rituals.

(28) Spelled Chin Lee prior to 1941.

(29) Personal communication: (July, 1973), Editha L. Watson, Mentmore, New Mexico.

(30) Letter communication: (November 12, 1974), John Rieffer, Wide Ruins, Arizona.

(31) Hannum (1958).

(32) Sallie (Lippincott) Wagner reported to the author that during their stay in California they sold out to a man named Carl Hine (1942), but reaquired the property two years later by repossession. Personal communication: (March 11, 1975), Santa Fe, New Mexico.

(33) Hannum (1944).

(34) Hegemann (1963), p. 173.

(35) Letter communication: (November 23, 1973), Paul Babbitt, Jr., Babbitt Brothers Trading Company, Flagstaff, Arizona.

(36) The four sacred mountains of Navajo mythology are: East: *Sisnaajini* (Sierra Blanca, Colorado); West: *Doko'ooaliid* (San Francisco Peak, Arizona); North: *Dibentsaa* (Mount Hesperus, Colorado); South: *Tsoodzil* (Mount Taylor, New Mexico).

(37) Hegemann (1963), p. 302.

(38) Amsden (1934), p. 213.

(39) Amsden (1934), pp. 52-53.

(40) Referred to in some writings as "double cloth," or "double-faced" cloth.

Bibliography

Adair, John, 1944, The Navajo And Pueblo Silver-smiths: Norman, Okla., Univ. of Okla. Press.

Amsden, Charles Avery, 1964, Navajo Weaving, Its Technic And Its History: Glorieta, N. Mex., Rio Grande Press (Reprint).

Bahti, Tom, 1966, Introduction To Southwestern Indian Arts & Crafts: Flagstaff, Ariz., K. C. Publications.

Bennett, Noël and Bighorse, Tiana, 1971, Working With The Wool: Flagstaff, Ariz., Northland Press.

Bennett, Noël, 1974, The Weaver's Pathway, Flagstaff, Ariz., Northland Press.

Bryan, Nonobah and Young, Stella, 1940, Native Navajo Dyes: Washington, D.C., U.S. Dept. Interior.

Burbank, E. A., 1944, Burbank Among The Indians: Caldwell, Idaho, Caxton Printers, LTD.

Coolidge, Dane and Mary, 1930, The Navajo Indians: Boston, Mass., and New York, N.Y.; Houghton Mifflin Co.

DeLauer, Marjel, 1975, A Century of Indian Traders And Trading Posts: Phoenix, Ariz., Arizona Highways Magazine, March, Vol. LI, No. 3.

Dutton, Bertha, 1961, Navajo Weaving Today: Santa Fe, New Mex., Museum of N. Mex. Press.

Eckel, LaCharles Goodman, 1934, History of Ganado, Arizona: Flagstaff, Ariz., Museum of Northern Arizona; Vol. VI, No. 10.

Gillmor, Francis, and Wetherill, Louisa Wade, 1952, Traders To The Navajo: Albuquerque, N. Mex., Univ. of N. Mex. Press.

Gilpin, Laura, 1971, The Enduring Navajo: Austin, Tex., Univ. of Texas Press.

Granger, Byrd H. (ed.), 1960, Arizona Place Names: Tucson, Ariz., Univ. of Ariz. Press.

Hannum, Alberta, 1958, Paint The Wind: New York, N.Y., The Viking Press.

Hannum, Alberta, 1944, Spin A Silver Dollar: The Story of A Desert Trading Post: New York, N.Y., The Viking Press.

Hegemann, Elizabeth Compton, 1963, Navajo Trading Days: Albuquerque, N. Mex., Univ. of N. Mex. Press.

Hill, Willard W., 1948, Navajo Trading And Trading Ritual, A Study of Cultural Dynamics; Southwestern Journal of Anthropology, Vol. IV, No. 4.

Hollister, U.S., 1972, The Navajo And His Blanket: Glorieta, N. Mex., Rio Grande Press (Reprint).

Hubbell, Lorenzo, 1930, Fifty Years An Indian Trader: Touring Topics, Vol. XXII, No. 12.

James, George Wharton, 1970, Indian Blankets And Their Makers: Glorieta, N. Mex., Rio Grande Press (Reprint).

James, H. L., 1973, Navajo Rugs-The Regional Style: Socorro, N. Mex., N. Mex. Geological Society Guidebook, Monument Valley, 24th Field Conference.

James, H. L., 1974, The Romance of Navajo Weaving: Santa Fe, N. Mex., New Mexico Magazine, January/February, Vol. 52.

Jeffers, Jo, 1967, Hubbell Trading Post National Historic Site: Phoenix, Ariz., Arizona Highways Magazine, September, Vol. XLIII.

Kahlenberg, Mary Hunt and Berlant, Anthony, 1972, The Navajo Blanket: Los Angeles, Calif., Praeger Publishing Co.

Kent, Kate Peck, 1961, The Story of Navajo Weaving: Phoenix, Ariz., Heard Museum.

Kluckhohn, Clyde, and Leighton, Dorothea, 1962, The Navajo: Garden City, N.Y., Doubleday Publishing Co.

Leighton, Alexander H., and Dorothea C., 1945, The Navajo Door: Cambridge, Mass., Harvard Univ. Press.

Lesch, Alma, 1970, Vegetable Dyeing: New York, N.Y., Watson-Guptill Publishing Co.

Luomala, Katherine, 1974, Navajo Weaving: Santa Fe, N. Mex., El Palacio Quarterly, Vol. 80, No. 1; Museum of N. Mex. Press.

Matthews, Washington, 1882, Navajo Weavers, Washington, D.C., Bureau of American Ethnology, Third Annual Report.

Matthews, Washington, 1968, Navaho Weavers & Silversmiths: Palmer Lake, Colo. (Reprint).

Matthews, Washington, 1902, The Night Chant, A Navajo Ceremony: Washington, D.C., Memoirs of The American Museum of Natural History, Vol. VI.

Maxwell, Gilbert S., 1963, Navajo Rugs — Past, Present And Future: Palm Desert, Calif., Best-West Publications.

McNitt, Frank, 1959, Two Gray Hills — America's Costliest Rugs: Santa Fe, N. Mex., New Mexico Magazine, April, Vol. 37.

McNitt, Frank, 1962, The Indian Traders: Norman, Oklahoma, Univ. of Okla. Press.

McNitt, Frank, (ed.), 1964, Navajo Expedition: Norman, Oklahoma, Univ. of Okla. Press. (Reprint).

McNitt, Frank, 1972, Navajo Wars: Albuquerque, N. Mex., Univ. of N. Mex. Press.

Mera, H. P., 1949, Navajo Textile Arts: Santa Fe, N. Mex., Laboratory of Anthropology.

Miller, Marjorie, 1972, Indian Arts And Crafts: Los Angeles, Calif., Nash Publishing Co.

Mills, George, 1959, Navaho Art And Culture: Colorado Springs, Colo., Taylor Museum Fine Arts Center.

Moore, J. B., 1911, The Navajo: Denver, Colo., Williamson-Haffner Co.

Mott, Dorothy Challis, 1931, Don Lorenzo Hubbell of Ganado: Tucson, Ariz., Arizona Historical Review, Vol. IV, No. 1.

Mullan, Read, 1964, Gallery of Western Art: Phoenix, Ariz., Read Mullan.

Newcomb, Franc Johnson, 1964, Hosteen Klah: Norman, Okla., Univ. of Okla. Press.

Newcomb, Franc Johnson, 1966, Navajo Neighbors: Norman, Okla., Univ. of Okla. Press.

Pearce, T. M. (ed.), 1965, New Mexico Place Names: Albuquerque, N. Mex., Univ. of New Mexico Press.

Pendleton, Mary, 1974, Navajo And Hopi Weaving Techniques: New York, Collier Books.

Reichard, Gladys A., 1939, Dezba: Woman of The Desert: New York, N.Y., J. J. Augustin.

Reichard, Gladys A., 1968, Navajo Shepherd And Weaver: Glorieta, N. Mex., Rio Grande Press (Reprint).

Reichard, Gladys A., 1968, Spider Woman: Glorieta, N. Mex., Rio Grande Press (Reprint).

Simpson, James H., 1850, Reconnaissance Expedition Into The Navajo Country, Senate Document No. 64, Washington, D.C.

Spiegelberg, A. F., 1925, Navajo Blankets: Santa Fe, N. Mex., El Palacio Quarterly, Vol. 18, Nos. 10 and 11: Museum of N. Mex. Press.

Tanner, Clara Lee, 1964, Modern Navajo Weaving: Phoenix, Ariz., Arizona Highways Magazine, September, Vol. XL.

Tanner, Clara Lee, 1968, Southwest Indian Craft Arts: Tucson, Ariz., Univ. of Arizona Press.

Twitchell, Ralph Emerson, 1963, The Leading Facts of New Mexico History: Albuquerque, N. Mex., Horn & Wallace.

Underhill, Ruth M., 1953, Here Come The Navajo: Lawrence, Ka., Haskell Institute — U.S. Indian Service.

Underhill, Ruth, 1944, Pueblo Crafts: Lawrence, Ka., Haskell Institute.

Underhill, Ruth M., 1956, The Navajo: Norman, Okla., Univ. of Okla. Press.

Utley, Robert M., 1961, The Reservation Trader In Navajo History: Santa Fe, N. Mex., El Palacio Quarterly, Vol. LXVIII, No. 1.

Watson, Editha L., 1957, Navajo Rugs: Phoenix, Ariz., Arizona Highways Magazine, August, Vol. XXXIII, No. 8.

Wheat, Joe Ben, 1974, Three Centuries of Navajo Weaving: Phoenix, Ariz., Arizona Highways Magazine, July, Vol. L., No. 7.

Winslowe, John R., 1969, Navajo Traders For Many Moons: True West Magazine, March-April, Vol. 16.

Whiteford, Andrew H., 1970, Indian Arts: New York, N.Y., Golden Press.

Whiteford, Andrew Hunter, 1970, North American Indian Arts: New York, N.Y., Western Publishing Co.

Pertinent titles issued by the Laboratory of Anthropology, Technological Series, Santa Fe, N. Mex.

Navajo Blankets of the Classic Period: 1938, Bulletin No. 3.

The Slave Blanket: 1938, Bulletin No. 5.

Pictorial Blankets: 1938, Bulletin No. 6.

Wedge Weave Blankets: 1939, Bulletin No. 9.

The Zoning Treatment in Navajo Blanket Design: 1940, Bulletin No. 12.

The Chinlee Rug: 1942, Bulletin No. 13.

Navajo Twilled Weaving: 1943, Bulletin No. 14.

Navajo Woven Dresses: 1943, Bulletin No. 15.

Cloth Strip Blankets of the Navajo: 1945, Bulletin No. 16.

Index